Calmfidence

Calmfidence

How to Trust Yourself,
Tame Your Inner Critic,
and Shine in Any Spotlight

PATRICIA STARK

BOULDER, COLORADO

© 2021 Patricia Stark

Sounds True is a trademark of Sounds True, Inc.

Published 2021

Cover design by Jennifer Miles
Book design by Meredith March

Printed in Canada

Library of Congress Cataloging-in-Publication Data

Names: Stark, Patricia, author.
Title: Calmfidence : how to trust yourself, tame your inner critic, and
   shine in any spotlight / Patricia Stark.
Description: Boulder, CO : Sounds True, 2021.
Identifiers: LCCN 2020056392 (print) | LCCN 2020056393 (ebook) | ISBN
   9781683647409 (hardback) | ISBN 9781683647416 (ebook)
Subjects: LCSH: Self-confidence. | Self-acceptance. | Calmness. |
   Criticism, Personal.
Classification: LCC BF575.S39 S73 2021 (print) | LCC BF575.S39 (ebook) |
   DDC 155.2–dc23
LC record available at https://lccn.loc.gov/2020056392
LC ebook record available at https://lccn.loc.gov/2020056393

10 9 8 7 6 5 4 3 2 1

Contents

Part Four: Natural Calmfidence

"It is important to remember
that we all have magic inside us."

J. K. Rowling

INTRODUCTION

A Magical and Powerful Combination

Working with more than two thousand clients and students over the past eighteen years to help them find their comfort zone in public speaking and performing on stage and in front of the camera, I've learned that everyone (yes, everyone) has their own struggles with "letting themselves shine in the spotlight." Everyone experiences anxiety and stress. Everyone has doubts and fears. It doesn't matter who you are, how old you are, or what you have achieved. I've trained celebrities, CEOs, supermodels, sports figures, physicians, psychologists, news anchors, TV hosts, authors, and wealthy entrepreneurs—highly successful people who you might assume have their act together all the time and an abundance of confidence in everything they do. But for most, I've found the journey still isn't easy. Many have cried in my training room as they faced their personal doubts and fears.

Big, burly, well-known athletes have shed tears during private sessions with me as I coached them on how to present themselves in front of a camera for the first time. They put so much pressure on themselves to perform as well on camera as they do on the field, and they tend to forget that proficiency takes some practice. Beautiful models whose faces grace fashion magazines have sat with me, full of insecurity and self-doubt from years of being judged only by their physical appearances. A successful lawyer whose mother was harshly critical of her throughout her life struggled with feelings that she would never be good enough, even as she was given her own interview show by a national media outlet. A network television chef whose father would have preferred she become a doctor grappled to free herself from his disappointment as she pictured him judging her through the lens while she shared her recipes on her successful cooking show.

I began to realize that everyone I worked with had two things in common: they wanted to learn to find their *calm* in stressful or unknown situations, and they wanted to be able to trust themselves to communicate with *confidence* inside and out (in their self-talk and to the world around them). That's when I was struck with the concept of *Calmfidence*. I believe that the duo of calm and confidence is something that everyone (not just presenters and performers) wants and needs in their everyday lives. Confidence is important. But calm and confidence together is a magical and powerful combination. Calmfidence shapes your life. When you are calm you make better choices. You can think straight. You're in the driver's seat. You trust yourself, and others trust your judgment. Calmfidence is the steady, quiet, inner thread of self-reliance and self-knowledge that holds you together when the outside world is in a whirl. People who lack Calmfidence struggle with people skills, communication skills, and leadership skills. It's hard to relate to other people when you're self-conscious or stressed out. When we are overly self-aware and hyper-focused on ourselves, we can't focus on the needs of others. When we are agitated, or we're rushing and letting the pressure get to us, we are not in charge of ourselves and cannot lead others. When you have Calmfidence, you treat yourself better, and, in turn, you treat others better.

Calmfidence is contagious. People can feel it. It sets the tone. People want to be around people who exude it. Calmfidence is what's needed in most situations. And, isn't Calmfidence what we all want and need from the people we rely on, like our doctor, airplane pilot, teacher, coach, babysitter, and even dog walker?

I know firsthand what it's like to struggle with anxiety, doubt, and fear. When I was younger I didn't have Calmfidence, and I've never forgotten how paralyzing it was. Growing up and through my college years, whenever I was called on in class, my heart would pound and sweat would pour down the sides of my body. Even when I knew the answer and wanted to raise my hand, I would get anxious and sweaty, and I wouldn't dare speak up. I couldn't walk up to the lunch line past all the tables of students without bringing a friend. I was introverted, nervous, scared, and I didn't know how to socialize well, which affected my schoolwork, my jobs, and my relationships. Looking back on my own Calmfidence journey, I can tell you that that is exactly what it was: a journey. Real change happens incrementally, a little bit at a time. It's been a series of small steps and experiences that have built a solid foundation of calm confidence that is now at the core of my life.

Through coaching and training thousands of my clients and students, I've found that everyone has the ability to work through their obstacles and successfully create their own personal foundation of Calmfidence. This can happen for you, too.

Calmfidence Inside and Out

Being a confident communicator helps you connect with others and with the world around you. A great communicator also learns to be a great listener. You become more curious and more interested in others. You become less self-focused and more other-focused. This in turn makes you less self-conscious and less hung up on worrying about how you look and sound.

Pursuing a career in front of the camera, you have to learn to stop taking things personally, which is generally pretty good advice for working in most careers. You are turned down regularly when you go to auditions, and in other businesses you get turned down in other ways, but you have to persist. I got used to hearing the word no and not letting it stop me. My life became the old Japanese proverb "fall down seven times, stand up eight." I also became an avid reader of personal development books and biographies of people I admired, finally understanding that I had as much right as anyone else in this world to ask for what I wanted and go for it. I started to really pay attention to the stories I was telling myself about myself. I learned that the most important thing you will ever hear is what you say to yourself.

Calmfidence doesn't come from what happens *to you*; it comes from what happens *in you*. So I created my own personal confidence-building regimen (which I now share with my clients and students), and once I started to be calmer and more confident, my whole world changed. The way people responded to me changed. The way *I* responded to me changed.

Work and relationships and life became so much more positive and fulfilling. I remember the first time I felt at peace and powerful when I was very much outside of my comfort zone, putting myself out there in a way I had never done before. I was invited to be a guest on a PBS network show in New Jersey. It was my first television interview where the tables were turned and I was now the guest being interviewed rather than the host or anchor conducting the interview. The topic was public-speaking fear and how to overcome it. When the producers told me I would be introduced as a "communication expert," the impostor syndrome kicked in big time! The description sounded terribly self-important. It suddenly flashed through my mind, *What if the so-called communication expert makes a mistake communicating during the interview?* Was I expected to be a shining example of perfect communication skills? Just as doubt and fear were about to take hold, I suddenly felt a tremendous feeling of both calm and confidence come over me. Calmfidence! There it was! I felt calm because I realized I was there to help, to be of service. To give viewers some tips to overcome their own fears. It wasn't about me being perfect. It wasn't about me at all. I was confident because I had been helping people improve their communication skills for a long time and I knew it had made a difference in their lives. I got really excited by this new perspective, and the interview went very well (and led to many more).

I've seen this shift happen with so many of my clients over the years, and it's really amazing to witness how freeing it is. Watching my clients and students soar and succeed with their own personal Calmfidence is the most fulfilling part of my work. It might sound silly, but my work has actually become sacred for me. It's an incredible privilege to help people find their voice and shine their light in this world. My hope is that you can create your own personalized inner Calmfidence using the proven techniques, natural remedies, relaxation exercises, communication skills, and mindset shifts outlined in this book. Whether you need to conquer your fear of public speaking, ace a job interview, convince colleagues of the importance of a plan or project, promote your business through television or video, create a career in front of the camera, give a TED talk, sound more confident over the phone, or just become more calm and confident throughout all aspects of your life, *Calmfidence* will help you to trust yourself to handle any situation.

How to Use This Book to Create Calmfidence Daily and When You Find Yourself in the Spotlight

This book is a toolbox for building your own Calmfidence. It's filled with golden nuggets of tips, how-to advice, and clients' stories that you can apply to the many situations and stages in your life. It's a collection of wisdom, strategies, light-bulb moments, exercises, and best practices that both my clients and I have learned and used over the past two decades. You don't have to read the book straight through; I encourage you to jump around and search for the types of Calmfidence that you want to apply to what's happening in your personal or work life right now. You may find helpful reminders of tips you already know. You may even surprise yourself and open this book to a random page now and then, like finding a daily Calmfidence fortune cookie. If you do choose to read this book from beginning to end, you'll find that it's a nice progression, starting with ways you can create a solid foundation of Calmfidence in general, followed by ways to strengthen your calm and confidence during more stressful and challenging times, moving on to strengthening your communication skills and interpersonal skills, and then wrapping up with plenty of tangible tips and even some fun and delicious things you can try on for size.

There are four main parts to this book. Part 1, "Everyday Calmfidence," focuses on mindset strategies to boost your Calmfidence. I show you how to deal with or eliminate Calmfidence killers, provide self-care recommendations, and give you Calmfidence tools you can use to create Calmfidence daily.

Part 2, "Resilient Calmfidence," focuses on times when you find yourself on shaky ground, with tips and strategies to handle setbacks, find your courage and grit, and pursue your goals and dreams with Calmfidence.

Part 3, "Communication Calmfidence," focuses on an abundance of ways you can build self-trust in both your internal and external communication skills and interpersonal skills. I have included strategies for more positive powerful self-talk, improving your speaking voice, confident eye-contact tips, and empowering nonverbal communication skills like facial expression and body language, right through to successfully handling that big speech or interview.

And finally, part 4 focuses on "Natural Calmfidence," with a cornucopia of tips and remedies found in nature that ease stress and anxiety, increase calm, and help with sleep, as well as mental and physical exercises that you can use to create Calmfidence instantly.

When you gain control over your calm and confidence, you control your destiny. When you build Calmfidence in every area of your life, and in every imaginable and unexpected situation, you will:

- See more opportunities that you didn't notice before.
- Have a positive energy that others will respond to even before you open your mouth.
- Develop a quiet, still, strong foundation on which to base your choices and decisions.
- Have more direction when setting goals.
- Trust yourself.
- Celebrate life instead of being afraid.
- Create your life rather than waiting for others to do it for you.

Whether it's confidence when speaking in front of others or quieting the mind's inner critic, it all comes down to being able to tap into a place of calm—in the moment, in the situation, and during the discussion or challenge at hand. Calmfidence isn't something we're born with; it's learned, and, more importantly, it's earned. This book contains a lot of information, but I encourage you to use the parts that you feel you need right now. Some things may not apply to you until another time or opportunity. Remember, creating Calmfidence is a process. Inner Calmfidence means different things to different people. It's your own definition of what gives you peace of mind and the feeling that you are able to depend on yourself. It's when you know in your core that *you've got this*. It's when you know that things will be okay, and even if for some reason they won't, you'll make it work, and *you'll* be okay. Calmfidence is a muscle—you can build it and strengthen it, and not just for yourself, but also to lift up those around you and in your community. So let's get started!

Part One

Everyday Calmfidence

1

Calmfidence Boosters

Every morning starts a new page in your
story. Make it a great one today.

Doe Zantamata

Wouldn't it be wonderful to feel calm and confident every day, no matter what was happening in your life or what was going on in the world around you? I think we all know that really isn't realistic for most of us, unless you are a yogi living in an ashram, the Dalai Lama, or maybe Deepak Chopra. The rest of us have to consciously create ways to give ourselves a boost of calm and confidence daily. Like brushing our teeth and showering, it's something we should aim for every day if we want to begin with a fresh start each morning. But it's not always that easy. It's especially hard if you are going through a stressful time in your life or have an upcoming event that you're feeling very anxious about. I think it's important here to really define what I mean by the word *calm* in Calmfidence. It's not a mellow, low-energy, emotionless type of calm where you don't have a worry in the world. It's an energizing calm that helps you feel more balanced and sure of yourself. The good news is, there are a lot of things we can do to create this type of calm and confidence in our daily lives. Start with checking in on your baseline—your state of Calmfidence each morning.

State of Calmfidence

What state of mind do you generally live in? Each day can start out very differently depending on what's happening in our life and how we're feeling about it. Our state of Calmfidence will affect how we show up each day for our family, our work, our friends, and, most importantly, ourselves. Most of the time we get up and go through the motions; we let the day run us instead of us running our day—or worse, we launch into our day with a form of dread, anticipating stress or even just a general sense of anxiety. Think of the last time you were super calm and confident. How did it feel? How did your body feel? Were you standing tall? Was your attitude unstoppable? Did you take charge and just know what you had to do and why you had to do it? What if you could do something that could bring you back to that empowered place on a daily basis, especially when things aren't going so well? Tuning into your state of Calmfidence each morning can help you tap into a self-awareness that can influence the kind of day you will have. A self–check-in like this is the first step to implementing Calmfidence boosters that can help you to remember how to find your balance and gain a sense of control over the day. Each morning, ask yourself:

- Do I feel balanced, or overwhelmed?
- Am I feeling encouraged, or am I discouraged?
- Is my energy positive, or negative?
- Do I feel in control, or out of control?
- Do I want to feel the way I am feeling? If not, what actions can I take to feel differently?

A Boost of Proof

There's so much research on how we can support and boost our calm and confidence. Universities, medical journals, and health and wellness reports are full of scientific proof that show our thoughts, choices, and actions can have a direct impact on our body, mind, and spirit in either a positive or negative way. We are in the driver's seat. We can grow, change, and transform no matter what our age or stage of life. But all the proof in the world means nothing if we do not actively *choose* to boost! We cannot always control what happens to us, but we can always choose how we are going to respond to it. Calmfidence boosters help you create a foundation of inner strength, wisdom, and self-trust.

BOOST #1: CHECK YOUR FOCUS

What we focus on expands. What we focus on becomes our reality. We have all faced many challenges over the past few years: a pandemic, social unrest, recession, job insecurity, and lack of health care among them. Consumer confidence, confidence in our country and government, and confidence in ourselves are put to the test daily. Essentially, our lives, our work, and our purpose all boil down to what we choose to focus on. We can choose to focus on the positive or the negative. Yes, we should be informed. Yes, we should be concerned about others. But if we let ourselves be inundated, overwhelmed, and broken down by bad news, we cannot focus on cultivating and strengthening our own lives and resources. The world goes on around us, but we all actually create our own little personal universe each and every day.

American philosopher Ralph Waldo Emerson was known to say in his lectures and essays, "A man is what he thinks about all day long." I have found this to be true. Of course, we cannot and should not minimize our need to focus on a serious or troubling situation. But if it is our only focus, it will consume us. Each day, check your focus by giving your attention to what is going right. Focus on solutions to problems, not just the problems. Focus on what is good. Focus on DOING good. Be aware of the things that are trying to catch your focus as well. We are constantly bombarded by people, media, social media, advertising, and a world that says "look here!" There are so many things competing for our attention, and many of them do not serve us well. Choose wisely. Be careful who and what you give away your precious focus to. So often we also give away our time by focusing too much on other people's lives. We turn away from investing in ourselves and appreciating our own lives and spend hours watching how others live on social media, on television, and in magazines. Protect your focus as if it were gold because it truly is priceless. Shift your focus to the good stuff. Look for good news. Focus on things that encourage you, like uplifting stories, positive people, empowering books, websites, movies, hobbies, and music. Focus on trying to look for the positive in yourself and everything around you. Remember, what you focus on expands. It becomes your reality.

Checking your focus boosts your calm by:

- Keeping you from feeling overwhelmed.
- Giving you a better sense of balancing the good against the bad.
- Creating a positive outlook that can help minimize stress and worry.

Checking your focus boosts your confidence by:

- Helping you be in control of where your attention goes.
- Helping you devote time to things that build you up and increase your sense of well-being.
- Helping you look for the good in yourself and in others.

BOOST #2: GRATITUDE CALMFIDENCE

The human brain cannot focus on both positive and negative thoughts at the same time, so you can't be grateful and anxious simultaneously. This means you can actually interrupt feelings of anxiety by focusing on something you are grateful for! According to a 2020 article in *Psychology Today*, research shows that gratitude can minimize stress, improve mental health, and increase positive thinking. Gratitude stimulates a part of the brain called the hypothalamus, which regulates anxiety. Once your brain starts looking for things to be grateful for, it begins to notice more and more things to be grateful for. You will actually attract more positive things into your life. So start off each morning and pick a few things you can be grateful for. Maybe it's just as simple as being grateful that you get a brand new day to start fresh, that you can see the sunrise or smell a warm cup of coffee. End each day with gratitude (even if it wasn't a great one) thinking about at least one thing you can be grateful for. Practicing a nightly gratitude ritual can even help you sleep better. When you have gratitude for what you already have, no matter how small, it opens the door for the bigger things that you want more of in your life. Most of all it's having gratitude for where we are right now. Gratitude for what we've got right now: the good, the bad, and the ugly. Because this is it—your life is happening right here, right now. Gratitude is what makes people truly happy.

Having gratitude boosts your calm by:

- Minimizing stress.
- Increasing feelings of happiness.

Having gratitude boosts your confidence by:

- Helping you appreciate who you are and what you have right now.
- Increasing positive feelings of self-esteem and self-sufficiency.
- Increasing feelings of value and self-worth.

BOOST #3: HAPPY CALMFIDENCE

How happy are you on a daily basis? Research shows that happy emotions increase wellness, confidence, energy, and longevity. Happiness expands your vision of what is possible with hope, expectation, and enthusiasm. Negativity narrows your vision. People generally are poor predictors of what they think will make them happy. "I'll be happy once I _____." You fill in the blank. So often we do this. We hold our happiness hostage until a later date, some vague time in the future when all the stars align and we finally get all the stuff we want and all the circumstances we want unfold just perfectly. But that day never seems to come because there will always be some new thing we want, a new goal, or some new obstacle in our way. Sure, things, experiences, goals, and achievements will give you boosts of happiness when you attain them, but many times they are short-lived and it's back to reality. The only time you can choose to be happy is right here and now. Abraham Lincoln said, "We are as happy as we make up our mind to be." When you make a conscious decision to choose joy right now, so many things change. You change. You don't have to be over-the-top happy every day, either. How about happy enough? It's not a constant state. Try to incorporate happy moments here and there. Sprinkle in little things that bring you a smile or maybe bring someone else in your life a smile. A 2012 study by the Association for Psychological Science showed that smiling actually changes your mood. It's a mind-body connection trigger. Even if you don't feel like it, putting on a smile can alter your state of mind. Anything you can do to influence it or take charge of your state of mind puts you in control. Smiling is also a universal language; it influences others around you, and you don't even have to say a word.

Choosing happiness boosts your calm by:

- Increasing feelings of joy in your life.
- Minimizing negativity.

Choosing happiness boosts your confidence by:

- Knowing you get to decide your own personal definition of happiness—not someone else or something else.
- Knowing that you are the only one who can truly make yourself happy frees you from depending on others to find it.
- Making the most of each moment and not delaying feelings of happiness.

BOOST #4: GROWTH MINDSET CALMFIDENCE

Most stress and anxiety come from a feeling of being stuck. Often this is due to having a fixed mindset. A fixed mindset is the belief that things can't or won't change or that we can't or won't change. A fixed mindset usually develops over time. It can take hold from the way we were raised, by how others defined us, or from the people we hang out with. It can come from a bad experience that we feel has left us scarred or affected in some way that we cannot change. When you have a fixed mindset you tend to believe you are born with a certain level of talent, ability, and even intelligence and that it does not change. A fixed mindset can lead to feelings of hopelessness and discouragement. When we shift to a growth mindset, we are now giving ourselves permission to change, learn, grow, and evolve. Hope and expectation are two of the most important things we can have to keep us from getting discouraged and feeling defeated. When we have a growth mindset we feel we can keep advancing. Rather than believing that our traits and abilities are fixed, a growth mindset helps us see that we can continue to learn and grow all throughout our lives. Even when we have experienced an injustice, a tragedy, or a huge disappointment, when we shift our perspective to a growth mindset our brain starts to look for ways to turn those negative experiences into something positive that can help us or to be used to help others. An example of this would be when a client says to me, "I am not a confident person" or "I can't do this!" I immediately begin to get them to change their statements to "I'm working to increase my confidence" or "I can do this if I work hard and learn new skills." When a person insists that "This is just the way that I am" or "I'm too old to change," they are literally locking themselves into being stuck. Yet when other people truly believe that they can reinvent themselves at any point in their life, their mindset works to make that true. Start to think of yourself as a lifelong learner. Be as open-minded as possible. Know that you can change yourself and change your circumstances if you can start to believe it's possible. Each day ask yourself:

- What can I learn today?
- How can I improve?
- What do I have the power to change right now?
- Are my beliefs about myself really true or have I just accepted what someone else or what society has told me?
- How have my challenges made me stronger?
- How can my experiences help others?

Choosing to have a growth mindset boosts your calm by:

- Helping you feel that you are no longer stuck.
- Increasing your level of patience and compassion for yourself.

Choosing to have a growth mindset boosts your confidence by:

- Helping you know that you can keep fine tuning, keep improving.

- Knowing that hard work and persistence are an important part of developing talent.

- Learning that challenges and struggles are needed for growth.

- Giving you determination and perseverance.

BOOST #5: CALMFIDENCE COMPARTMENTS

No one can live yesterday, today, and tomorrow all at once and stay calm and confident. Dale Carnegie wrote of the notion of living in "day-tight compartments." That essentially means blocking yourself off from everything but the day at hand. It is overwhelming to live life in the past, present, and future simultaneously. Yesterday is gone. It cannot be changed. Let go of past mistakes and failures. Don't talk about them. Don't think about them. And tomorrow does not exist yet. The only reality is right here, right now. No matter how stressful, bad, or upsetting a day is, most individuals can make it from morning till night if they just deal with what's happening on that day without adding yesterday and tomorrow into the equation.

I've taken this a step further in my own life and with my clients by editing it down into even more digestible chunks and attempting to deal with life in hour-tight and minute-tight compartments. I recommend breaking down days and moments into segments, with a time and place separate from the rest. I have clients who used to wake up every morning with knots in their stomachs from thinking about a speech that is two weeks away. Other clients spent days dreading an interview that would only take fifteen minutes or a TV appearance that would last three minutes. The buildup is worse than the actual event could ever be. The anticipation was literally making them sick. They lived the event in their mind many times before it happened, and usually in a negative light, only visualizing all that could go wrong.

I helped them to get out their calendar and select chunks of time to plan ahead and prepare, to visualize only what they want to have happen and when, and to see success instead of dread and worry. When they focus on things in smaller chunks, taking one step at a time, and pace themselves throughout each day, they stay calmer and feel a sense of control. And many times, they tell me they actually get more done in less time.

No matter what your day holds, you can do this, too. When you plan and fully digest small moments in time, do what you can, do the best that you can, then close up shop on the topic and move on to the next, you will get a better handle on both big and small things that normally would stress you out. You can outline and prioritize your day and decide what each time frame will focus on. You can even decide which time frame you will choose to express your anxiety if you wish but limit that time and stick to it. Using an egg timer or cell phone alarm to commit to the designated time frames to focus on one thing at a time works really well. By focusing on just what's in front of you hour by hour, and minute by minute, you are less likely to get overwhelmed, worry all day, or live in a negative anticipation of what's to come.

Compartmentalizing helps boost your calm by:

- Making your day easier to manage.
- Making worries more digestible and less overwhelming.

Compartmentalizing helps boost your confidence by:

- Knowing you can handle what's right in front of you.
- Helping you feel a better sense of control over your emotions and how and when you want to deal with things each day.

BOOST #6: SEIZE THE DAY CALMFIDENCE

In the movie *Dead Poets Society*, Robin Williams plays a teacher who gathers his students around a very old photo of a group of students from the same school. He explains to the current students that the group of boys in the photo all had hopes and dreams, passions and desires, but that their time is gone. They can no longer accomplish anything in this world. Their time is over. He begins to whisper "Seize the day, seize the day," as if the boys in the photo are calling out from beyond the grave through time and space saying, "You are here, you get to do it, you get to be there."

When you seize the day—in Latin, *carpe diem*—you boost your Calmfidence. What can you get done today? Why put it off? When you think about putting things off to another day, ask yourself if it would be okay if they never got done. This is a good barometer to play with. Don't die with that book in you. Don't die with your song in you. Don't die with your talent or idea never realized. What seed is planted in you? Is there something you have been dreaming about? Something you want to change or accomplish? When you pursue the thing that has been placed in your heart and mind, your confidence begins to soar.

There are many people who had goals they never realized. Many people who procrastinated or waited for the right time that never came. Then there are those who did achieve great things but ran out of time to do more. You get to be here right now. Calmfidence comes from being fully present in the current moments of your life. Here are some things to ponder:

* Each person on this planet gets the same number of hours in each day and the same number of days in each year. No one has more or less time than you. Anyone who has achieved anything great did it in the same allotted time that any of us are given in an average lifespan. Legendary people throughout history had to make use of the same twenty-four hours a day that are given to each of us while we are here on this earth.

* Each new day truly is a gift. A gift that is not given to everyone.

Remember and respect those who have gone before you. Who do you know who doesn't get to be here anymore? Family, friends, acquaintances, and people you only knew from a distance are no longer with us.

I've had a strange and wonderful experience over the past several years. When I was going through an extremely difficult time in my life, I began to feel the presence and see images in my mind's eye of two women from my past who had lost their young lives tragically. One died violently before she even had the chance to finish high school, a beautiful and friendly, talented artist who would have done amazing things in this world. The other was a wonderful, sweet young mother taken in her twenties by a terrible disease, who never got to see her daughter grow up. They would take turns just popping into my head during my darkest hours and days. At first, I wondered why I would randomly think of them. As it continues to happen during times of stress, overwhelm, or worry, I swear I hear them whisper, "But you get to be here." In those moments I reflect on their shortened lives and remember the times our paths crossed. I think of all the things they never got to experience. Perhaps it is my subconscious reminding me of something I know deep inside. But in my heart, I feel it is the vibrant spirits of two women who give me a gentle reminder that no matter how bad it seems . . . I get to be here.

How many things in your life do you say "I have to" to? I have to go to work today. I have to take care of my kids today. I have to _____ today. What if you changed those statements to "I get to" today? If you are healthy and have a job, then *you get* to go to work. If you are lucky enough to have been blessed with children, you *get to* take care of them, do stuff for them, or be with them today. If you want to lose weight or be in better shape, you *get to* work out and eat right if you are healthy and able to make those choices. If you have to give a speech, you are lucky that someone thinks enough of your knowledge that you *get to* share it with others. Try replacing "have to" with "get to" for a week and then for a month. Replace your inner dialogue and your outward comments to others using "I get to." You will be amazed at the difference this will make. You get to be here! Seize the day. It is yours.

Seizing the day helps boost your calm by:

- Minimizing the stress that comes from inaction.
- Helping you be fully present in the moment.

Seizing the day helps boost your confidence by:

- Motivating you to take action.
- Increasing your passion and enthusiasm for your goals and dreams.

BOOST #7: CALMFIDENCE PRICE CHECKER

When we create too much drama around a thing, it's hard to be calm and confident. How high of a price are you putting on situations you face? Are you making something into a much bigger deal than it actually is?

As human beings we're all pretty good at doing this. We dramatize, "awfulize," and make things life-or-death situations when they really are not.

A perfect example of this is when I videotape clients during media or public speaking training sessions. Often, we go through exercises to just warm up and they don't know I have the camera rolling. The stakes are not yet high in their minds because we're just having a conversation or rehearsal. They are relaxed, not feeling self-conscious, and generally they are just being themselves. But as soon as people know the camera is rolling and they are "on," the nerves kick in and so does the self-awareness and the desire for perfection, and their personal pressure ramps into high gear. The price they now put on the situation goes up, along with their blood pressure and adrenaline.

Check the "price tag" you're putting on things in your life and career. Compare it to other prices in your life. An extreme example I use with very nervous students is to ask them, "Would you rather be in your current situation (public speaking, a big audition, an interview, or speaking in front of a camera) or at the deathbed of a loved one?" Or "How about running from bullets trying to protect your loved ones in a war zone in places like we hear about on the news every day?" I know the question sounds morbid, but it puts thing into perspective pretty quickly for them—and they happily choose the current situation over the extreme example.

It's important to ask yourself questions to see how much something really matters to you in the scheme of your life.

Price checker questions to ask yourself:

- Will this matter in five years?
- Is this worth losing my health over?
- What's the worst that can happen? And, so what if it does?
- Who do I know who has worse problems than this?
- What am I basing my price on?

Checking your price helps boost your calm by:

- Putting things into a better perspective.
- Getting your adrenaline in check.

Checking your price helps boost your confidence by:

- Facing worst-case scenarios ahead of time to conquer your fear.
- Toning down unrealistic expectations.

BOOST #8: SPIRITUAL CALMFIDENCE

Many studies, including a 2012 Yeshiva University study and a University College London study, have shown that when people practice a religion or have a kind of spiritual practice, their lives become more positive, they become more hopeful, and they don't worry as much. And it doesn't matter what religion that is, by the way. Whatever your personal definition—God, the Universe, Higher Intelligence, Mother Nature, Source—it's a transforming thing to feel connected to something bigger than we are. A 2006 University of Texas study showed that faith and spirituality can help you live longer. Praying is a form of meditation. If you're a person of faith, or if you engage in a spiritual practice of any kind, it is a powerful tool for creating Calmfidence in your life. Handing things over to a higher power can help you unload and release your body and mind so you can relax or sleep. It also helps to relieve stress and anxiety when you know you're not alone in whatever unnerving situation you find yourself in, feeling that you can connect to and tap into a larger purpose. My own faith has carried me through many high-stress situations and has been a source of Calmfidence when I wasn't finding it in any other way.

Spiritual Calmfidence helps boost your calm by:

- Serving as a powerful form of meditation.
- Easing feelings of worry and anxiety.

Spiritual Calmfidence helps boost your confidence by:

- Helping you feel connected to something bigger than yourself.
- Giving you a sense of purpose and value.

BOOST #9: CREATE YOUR CALMFIDENCE T-E-A-M

You can create your own Calmfidence support system around you, what I call your Calmfidence T-E-A-M. Here's who should be on your team:

T—Teachers: parents, educators, experienced people in your field of choice. Knowledge givers. People who are compelled to share what they know and happy to help you learn.

E—Elevators: friends who build you up, not tear you down. Personal cheerleaders, people you can turn to when you need a lift!

A—Advancers: people who want to see you succeed. They want to help you advance in your career, achieve your goals, and help you become a better person. They empower you.

M—Mentors: people who have been there, done that. They have blazed the trail and want to show you how to do the same. Role models who are accessible to you and who are the kind of person you would like to be. People who are willing to take the time to show you what they have learned the hard way, so that you don't have to start from scratch. These are people who have the experience, Calmfidence, and desire to help others be strong and flourish.

Your Calmfidence T-E-A-M becomes a solid foundation that you can draw from, lean on, get lifted up by, and even get a good nudge from when you need one. We all need people in our lives who support us, root for us, encourage us, and build us up. We can't choose the family we are born into; hopefully they are our biggest cheerleaders, but sometimes they simply aren't or can't be because they are unhappy or unmotivated themselves. We *can* choose our friends and partners, lovers, and soul mates.

When you pick a friend, partner, or spouse as a member of your Calmfidence support group, keep in mind that you want the person you're picking to help you. Surround yourself with encouraging positive people whenever possible. They will be your greatest resource. Again, Calmfidence is contagious, and people with true Calmfidence celebrate your dreams with you.

Fitness experts tell us to get a workout buddy—a running partner or a walking partner—who will encourage us on the days we don't feel like exercising. Exercising is more fun and interesting when you do it with someone else. Could you imagine if the person you picked to work out with was discouraging, negative, lackluster, selfish, or mean-spirited?

You'd drop that workout partner in a heartbeat because you know there would be no way you could put up with that! Well, the same goes for your friends and your spouse or partner. They'll be at your side for the marathon of life, and if they aren't your biggest cheerleaders and you theirs, how will you ever go the distance and be the best you can be?

A building will crumble without a strong foundation. A tree can withstand great storms if it is flexible and its roots are strong—but if little bugs eat away at its foundation over time, it will come crashing down with a soft breeze. If the relationships in your life are not building you up, they are knocking you down, or keeping you down. If you can't change these relationships immediately, start slowly adding one positive, encouraging person at a time to your life. Eventually you will build your own support group that can be a foundation of strength for you, one that will build you up and away from others who knock you down. When you know you have people rooting for you, your Calmfidence will soar!

BOOST #10: MORNING HABITS TO OWN YOUR DAY WITH CALMFIDENCE

You can use this quick four-step process to take charge of your day or create your own plan. The important thing is to put a series of positive habits in place each day to help you actively decide how your day will go.

You Snooze, You Lose!

It's so toasty and warm in bed and I just need five more minutes! When you hit that snooze button, you are telling your subconscious, "I'm not ready; I don't want to tackle this day." You start your day by putting things off. Instead, set your clock for a designated wake-up time and stick to it. You'll launch into your day feeling more definite and in charge.

Set the Tone for Your Day

The first few things you do as you awaken lay the foundation for your day. Checking email and social media or watching the news before you even get out of bed can bombard you with information overload and take away the clean-slate feeling of a fresh new morning. It can make you feel dread before you clear your head! Resist the urge and replace this habit with a more empowering one like a brief meditation or prayer, listening to uplifting music, or spending a few minutes thinking of one or two things you are grateful for. One of my clients told me years ago that as they get out of bed they say the word *thank* as one foot hits the floor and *you* as the other foot hits the floor to acknowledge their gratitude for another day. I've gotten into this habit myself, and it literally makes you put your best foot forward stepping into the day.

Make the Shower an Inspirational Place

The warmth, cleansing, and invigoration help your body and mind emerge into a new day. It's the perfect time and place to visualize the day you want to have. Close your eyes and see your day going smoothly in your mind's eye. Envision the outcomes you want. Focus and create—don't wait to react to what the day may bring.

Plan Your Day by the Hour as Best You Can

Schedule in slots for YOU time. Be it exercise, a few moments of silence, a call or meeting with a friend, quality time with those you care about, or uninterrupted time for a project or chore, the more you plan out your day in compartments, the more likely you are able to get the things done that are important to you. Instead of saying, "I don't have time," replace it with "It's not a priority" and see how that feels. If that statement doesn't sit well with you, you'll know that it's one of the things you need to actively schedule in order to make it happen. Even if unexpected things derail your plan, you are more likely to work in some of the things you hoped to.

Incorporating some or all of these Calmfidence boosters can really make a difference in the calm and confidence you can create and carry with you throughout each day. It's worth the effort to work them into your life even if it seems hard at first. Don't try to attempt them all at once. Pick one booster that feels like it might be right for where you are in your life right now and commit to it every day for a week and see how it works for you. Then try another. Different combinations work for different people. Let's recap these keys to Calmfidence before you take the time to reflect on how they resonate with you personally in the following chapter, "Calmfidence Killers."

Calmfidence Boosters Checklist

- Do a self-check each morning.
- Choose your focus.
- Use gratitude to interrupt anxiety.
- Weave in little happy moments throughout your day.
- Choose to have a growth mindset.
- Compartmentalize your day.
- Seize the day.
- Check your price tag.
- Tap into your spirit.
- Create your Calmfidence T-E-A-M.
- Create positive morning habits to help you own your day.

A Client's Story

I met Lisa when she attended one of my Women's Calmfidence weekend workshops in New York City. She was a talented interior designer from Long Island with big goals. Lisa had made a few appearances on local morning shows and had dreams of writing books, styling celebrity homes, and maybe even hosting her own TV show one day. The problem was that she wasn't a very positive person. When she was engulfed in her work she felt her best, but when she tried to enjoy down time with friends it would always end up being a real *downer*.

After several private coaching sessions with Lisa, she revealed that her main group of friends were pretty miserable. The only goals they seemed to have were to drink wine, lots of it, gossip up a storm, and "keep things real for Lisa" with a million reasons why she'd never connect with high-profile clients or have the time to write a book. They'd been her friends for many years, but through the coaching sessions Lisa came to a decision: in order to boost her career and her confidence, she needed to create a Calmfidence T-E-A-M. Though she still occasionally got together with her old friends, she started making some new connections. She joined a chapter of a businesswomen's mastermind group that shared success ideas and resources for professional women and began making friends quickly. She spent some of her free time with a few members of the group hiking, kayaking, and eating out. The positive, goal-oriented women she now spent time with cheered her on and made her feel like the sky was the limit when it came to her goals.

Soon, Lisa landed a spectacular interior design project in the Hamptons for one of America's most famous recording artists. "I love the way the colors of the couch and carpet play off of the surf and sand through the windows overlooking the beach!" the client said. Lisa was pinching herself—this was her dream come true. "You are super talented, Lisa," the Hamptons recording artist told her. "I hope you'll come to our reveal party this weekend. You'll see a lot of familiar famous faces here, and I know they'll be thrilled to meet the person who created this stunning transformation! You're going to be in big demand!"

Calmfidence Booster Reflections

List three things that you are grateful for:

_____

_____

_____

List four people who you feel are part of or could become your
Calmfidence T-E-A-M:

_____

_____

_____

_____

List three small things that bring you happiness throughout your day:

_____

_____

_____

What are some positive morning habits or rituals you can start
your day with?

_____

_____

_____

2

Calmfidence Killers

On Mondays, Wednesdays, and Fridays I wake up thinking I'm the
greatest thing ever. On Tuesdays, Thursdays, and Saturdays I think I
suck and I haven't accomplished anything and that I better get to it and
that I'm a fake and a fraud. And on Sundays I don't think about it at all.

David Foster

We all have our own Calmfidence killers—bad habits and beliefs
that prevent us from feeling the calm and confidence we wish we
could attain. Society in itself can be a big Calmfidence killer. We are bombarded by images, by advertising, media, and products and services that
can make us feel that we are not enough or that we don't have enough.
Groups, institutions, cultures, and even our families and friends often tell
us what we should think and how we should look, believe, and act to fit
into their mold or agenda. We also create so many Calmfidence killers
in our own mind—many of them that are not even real. Self-doubt
and self-sabotaging behaviors kick in big time when we look outside of
ourselves to try to find our calm and confidence, until we realize that all
Calmfidence starts from *within*. It's like Dorothy's story in *The Wizard of
Oz* when she realizes she has had the power all along: she just needs to stop
listening to the distractions and all the external noise and trust herself.

You might find that your list of things that hold back your Calmfidence is long, but don't let it get you down or make you feel bad about

yourself. In fact, identifying and facing your Calmfidence killers can help you to own them so that they can no longer own you. Following are some of the most common Calmfidence killers I've witnessed and how to turn them around.

Calmfidence Killer #1: Shadow People

Shadow people are the "they" in our minds—What will *they* think? What will *they* say? What if *they* don't like me? What if *they* don't think I'm good enough? What if *they* laugh? They are the critics, who may be real people in our lives or entirely imaginary and based on our assumptions; fears; cultural and societal forces; and stereotypes we've bought into. We believe they are against us, judging us or, worse, rejecting us, and they cast a dark shadow that can kill our Calmfidence. Shadow people say no to us long before real people do. Think about it. How many times have you pictured people telling you no even before you have met them? I'm talking about that sales prospect, that interviewer, that potential significant other. We assume that people will turn us down or think the worst about us rather than the best. We hear their voices in our heads and see their disapproval in our minds. We also create shadow people who we think have much better lives than we do. We tend to minimize ourselves but maximize others. We picture strangers and acquaintances having the most amazing jobs, spouses, children, houses, vacations, and spending abilities. We assume they've got it all going on. But who really knows what's happening behind closed doors in other people's lives? My father-in-law worked in law enforcement for years. He always talked about how shocked people would be if they knew the raw truth about what goes on inside their neighbors' homes. Shadow people are imaginary bullies. They can be faceless and heartless, but *you* are the one who gives them life and power.

Several years ago, a national cable network sent two of its anchors, a man and a woman, to me for some on-camera training. They arrived for their session together. The woman entered my room with a big bright smile, great energy, and enthusiasm. The man came in looking intense, cranky, and defensive. I immediately liked the woman and wanted to help her. I didn't feel the same way about the guy. I just felt uncomfortable. After talking to the two of them for a while, it turned out that the woman had interpreted her company sending her for training as a sign that her managers thought she had great potential. Leading up to our meeting she had been envisioning all the ways I was going to help her improve her skills that would lead to more opportunities at the network. The man, in contrast, had built up this whole idea that this training must mean the producers didn't think he was very good and that he needed to be corrected or fixed in some way. He had been visualizing that I was going to chew him up and spit him out, only focusing on all the things he was doing wrong! What he didn't know was that the producers had told me they were sending me two of their most promising upcoming talents. Yet he had assumed the worst. His negative thinking affected how he carried himself and how he addressed me—and this in turn influenced my impression of him as soon as he entered the room, even before he said anything. After we cleared the air, he realized I was there *for* him, not against him. He turned out to be a great guy with a lot of potential, just as his network predicted.

How to turn around the shadow people Calmfidence killer:

- Picture your shadow people as welcoming friends and allies.
- When making assumptions, assume the best instead of the worst.
- Expect people you've never met to treat you with respect.
- Expect people you've never met to like you.
- Expect people to see that you have something to offer, that you are of value.
- Remind yourself that everyone is struggling with something and that they are almost always more concerned about their own lives than critiquing and judging you.

Calmfidence Killer #2: The Inner Critic

Your inner critic is a nasty tenant who lives like a squatter in the back of your mind. The inner critic talks to you in a way that you wouldn't dare talk to anyone. It is a thief, and its favorite thing to steal is your Calmfidence. How often do we allow our inner critic to influence the choices we make leading up to a big presentation, interview, meeting, conversation, or goal? The inner critic works in subtle ways to discourage us. It's a little voice of uncertainty. It whispers, *Who do you think you are? You're not good enough, smart enough, worthy enough, or attractive enough.* The strangest thing, though, about the inner critic is that it really is just . . . us. It's not a stranger, a monster, or some outside force we can't control. It's a part of us that is just scared and insecure. It's trying to protect us. Instead of listening to it and taking direction from it, talk to your inner critic with another voice that you have: your inner coach. How would you coach a friend through a tough time? How would you talk to them if they were afraid or doubting themselves? Talk to your inner critic the way you would try to encourage a dear friend. (We'll get into a lot more detail about these two voices in chapter 9, "The Inner Voice of Calmfidence.")

Here's how you can counteract the inner critic Calmfidence killer:

- Acknowledge it, let it speak, and then talk back to it the way you might calm a frightened child. Think of the way one of your favorite teachers or coaches would help you work through a tough problem, doubt, or fear.

- Understand that if you don't talk to yourself positively, your inner critic will talk to you negatively.

- Remind yourself that even though your inner critic wants to alert you to its concerns, you have wisdom, knowledge, and experience that you can choose to focus on instead.

- Remember that *everyone* has their own inner critic they have to deal with. No one is immune to this. Some people have just learned how to stop letting it get in their way, which means you can too!

Calmfidence Killer #3: Worry

My grandfather always told me there is only one place on Earth where no one has any problems: the cemetery. Whenever I was going through anxiety, heartbreak, or disappointment, he would remind me of this. Everyone has problems. Everyone is struggling at some point with something. Sometimes it seems easier to think about what can go wrong and what we don't want than to focus on what can go right and what we *do* want. Worrying takes no effort at all. When we worry and dwell on things, we deplete our energy, freeze in our tracks, and die a thousand little deaths as we kill our dreams or stress out our days. We are basically telling ourselves the untruth that we cannot handle what lies ahead. In a recent study conducted by the University of Pennsylvania analyzing the worry journals of men and women, on average 91.39 percent of participants' worries did *not* come true. And for the small percentage of worries that did come true, the participants reported that things turned out better than they anticipated. It's important to note that the study also showed that time spent worrying took up over 25 percent of the participants' days! These results show that we give away so much of our time to worry about things that almost never happen!

Even when bad things do happen, we have to believe that we have what it takes to deal with them. We have to trust that we will find a way to overcome them. We can handle this. It's probably not going to be as bad as we think, anyway.

Here's how you can counteract the excessive worry Calmfidence killer:

* Write down your worries in a journal or notebook. Keep track of them and see which ones actually come true.

* Practice mindfulness—concentrate on being in THIS moment 100 percent. When we worry, we are actually trying to live in a future moment that doesn't even exist yet.

* Think of the absolute worst-case scenario and how you would handle it if it did come true. Anything less that ends up happening will seem easier to deal with.

* Take action and then let go—decide what you can and can't do about the situation you are worrying about. Do what you can to deal with potential concerns, and for anything that is out of your control, remind yourself that worry will not help anyway.

- Share your worries with a trusted loved one, friend, or counselor. They may help you to see things from a better perspective. Sometimes it's just a relief to talk over worries with someone else rather than dwelling on them alone.

Calmfidence Killer #4: Perfectionism

So many of my clients and students get caught in the trap of perfectionism. It's easy to do, especially when you find yourself in the spotlight. The pressure we put on ourselves to do and say everything perfectly is enormous when we feel all eyes are on us. I've found that a lot of people believe they are truly not good enough at something unless they are perfect at it. This even includes *life* for many people! When we try to be perfect we leave no room for being human. Human beings simply are not perfect and never will be. When you focus on trying to be perfect, you can't get out of your own way. You get hung up, blocked, critical, and have unreasonable expectations. When you finally let go of trying to be perfect you will give yourself the flexibility to simply be GOOD. Studies show we don't like perfect people anyway! A study conducted by social psychologist Elliot Aronson showed that people who others perceived as *perfect* were much more likeable when they messed up, stumbled, or made mistakes. People feel that imperfection shows that you are down to earth, approachable, and genuine.

Here's how you can counteract the perfectionism Calmfidence killer:

- Give yourself permission to be human.
- Decide to be perfectly imperfect!
- When mistakes, foibles, or gaffes happen, don't be so hard on yourself.
- Learn to laugh at yourself. Don't take yourself so seriously.
- Know that when you like yourself, including your mistakes and imperfections, others will find you more likeable as well.
- Keep in mind that small mistakes can be endearing to others and can actually make you more socially attractive.

* Understand that the fear of making a mistake or of doing something wrong is the very thing that causes you to mess up.

Calmfidence Killer #5: Procrastination

Procrastination is debilitating. It is like pouring quick-drying cement all over your body and mind. When we are unsure of ourselves we keep putting things off until we think everything is just right, but nothing is ever just right.

I have a client who is very good on camera. She is a physician and health expert who would love to have her own television talk show. She is often interviewed on television news programs, and she collects clips of the shows so she can put together a video overview of her work to show to broadcast agents and casting people. She's had it edited many times now, but she feels it is never quite right. She has never sent it to anyone to look at. She says she doesn't want to make a bad first impression. It has to be just perfect. I'm starting to get the sense that she will never send it to anyone.

If we wait for everything to be perfect, for the right moment, it will never come. Just work on being ready and get good enough for the next step. Each level will get you to the next. Just work with what you've got right now.

Usually the anticipation of things is much worse than the actual reality of things. For instance, many people who fear public speaking put off preparing their speech or presentation. They live in fear and dread, or they claim they don't have time so they don't have to deal with it. Unfortunately, it's almost impossible to give a good presentation without solid preparation—and so it becomes a self-fulfilling prophecy. If they had just taken the time to prepare, they would be much more confident in their material. Sometimes we procrastinate because we are actually afraid of success. I know that sounds crazy, but I've had clients who keep putting things off that they know would help them to be successful because they worry that if they do end up getting the thing they want, maybe they really aren't ready for it. Maybe they don't think they deserve it or they worry that if they get the spotlight they seek, they will be "found out"—shown to be a fraud. Other times we procrastinate because it's just easier to do nothing.

We want to avoid the pain of doing the thing that will give us the gain. Our desire to avoid the pain is much greater than the pleasure we hope to get from the gain!

When it comes to our goals and our life's work, procrastination can give us a false sense of comfort as we avoid pain, until the regret becomes much more painful than the work or action we put off.

Here's how you can counteract the procrastination Calmfidence killer:

- Don't let your feelings dictate taking action—don't wait until you feel inspired or in the mood. Just get to it.

- Know that the first step truly is the most difficult. Once you get rolling, everything starts to flow.

- Try to remember times that you put things off because they seemed overwhelming or difficult and then didn't seem so bad once you got into it.

- If you know you are not good with self-imposed deadlines, get someone to hold you accountable and give you deadlines.

- Visualize what you will feel like once the thing is done.

- Remember that perfectionism can cause you to procrastinate. Stop aiming for perfection and go with *good enough*!

- Stop waiting for the time to be right, for everything to line up. This is an excuse we use to delay taking action. Just go for it!

Calmfidence Killer #6: Defining Yourself from the Outside

Calmfidence is an inside job. When you define yourself by referring to things outside of yourself, it's really hard to have Calmfidence in multiple areas of your life. You are not your job, you are not your finances, you are not your alma mater, and you are not your situation. The people and world around you will change, as will their opinions and beliefs about you. The truth of who you are can only be found inside your own heart, mind, and spirit.

One of the exercises I teach my clients is to define and remember their "red thread." Years ago, my grandfather told me a story he had heard about an old-time baseball player who talked about the significance of the red thread of a baseball. If you look closely at a baseball, you'll see that thin red stitches hold it together. Baseballs take a beating. They are hurled through the air by pitchers in excess of 100 miles per hour. They are hit so hard by bats that they fly clear out of a stadium. Yet with only a few exceptions that thin red thread holds them together. The baseball player spoke of his faith as being like that red thread in his life. It held him together under intense stress and pressure.

I ask my clients and students to think about what their red thread is. Maybe it's their faith. Maybe it's their goals and dreams. Maybe it's their family. Maybe it's their mission, purpose, or passion. Whatever it is to them, I ask them to remember their red thread when they need to hold it together when things get tough.

Criticism from an outside source can hurt us unless we hold steady to that inner thread that is of greater importance to us. The red thread helps us calm down as we put things into a better perspective and remember what is most important to us.

I was invited to train an international group of young entrepreneurs on their public speaking/presentation skills for a competition where they had to pitch their business ideas to get investors interested in backing them. They had a lot of great concepts, plans, and products, but one-third of their score was going to be based on how they communicated to the judging panel. It was a thrill to find ways to help them get their presentation skills up to snuff so that their passion for their business could shine through. There were other seminars going on at the event for other young entrepreneurs who did not make it to the final competition. Everywhere I went it felt like I was in the middle of a hotbed of dreamers, inventors, and trailblazers.

It was a beautiful day in South Beach, Florida. During a break I decided to take a stroll down the boardwalk along the ocean. As I walked, I noticed an older man wearing a gray suit and a young man wearing a black concert T-shirt walking and chatting a few steps in front of me. We were all going at the same pace so I couldn't help but overhear some of their conversation. As our walk progressed, I got the impression that the older gentleman was mentoring the young guy.

At one point I heard him say to the young man, "If you make this decision, my opinion of you will not change, but more importantly, if you make this decision will your opinion of you change?"

Wow, I thought to myself, *that's got to be just about the best advice I've ever heard.* It's a question we should all ask ourselves whenever we are about to make a decision. There are so many external things that we allow ourselves to be defined by. Yet our opinion of *ourselves* should truly be the foundation of how we live our lives.

How to turn around the Calmfidence killer of defining yourself from the outside:

* Before you worry about what other people will think of you, first be concerned about what you will think of yourself if you do or don't do something. How will it make you feel about yourself?

* Decide to have your own personal high standards for yourself. Strive to reach them just for you. You are the one who will wake up and look yourself in the face every morning.

* Do not hand over your power to outside sources like other people. People can only put you down if you let yourself believe that their opinions of you are more important than your opinion of yourself.

* When you believe in yourself, you will have more to give to others. If you work to have a strong positive sense of self you will even have more strength to help others.

Calmfidence Killer #7: Compare and Despair

When we compare ourselves to others, it sets us up for despair. When I speak to young students at schools and to teen groups it always makes me sad to hear how much young people today are comparing themselves to others. "Compare and despair" has been going on forever. I remember it well in middle school and high school, but social media has made it more intense than ever. Now you can bring practically the whole world into the privacy of your home or bedroom and just scroll for hours and days, comparing yourself to the images and lives of others on your cell phone or computer. Compare and despair gets magnified when we don't use the Calmfidence booster of a positive focus (see chapter 1). Of course, there's nothing wrong with being interested in other people. Admiring the fashion, beauty, talents, and lifestyles of others can inspire us and help us learn what we like and don't like for ourselves. But it becomes a problem when we do it through the lens of comparison.

How to turn around the Calmfidence killer of compare and despair:

- When you admire others, always be sure to admire something about yourself at the same time.

- Understand that comparing yourself to others is like the old adage of comparing apples to oranges. You can't equally compare yourself to anyone else. Everyone is unique.

- Check in with how you are feeling. If you are feeling bad about yourself while looking at what others are doing or what they look like, then you know you are catching yourself in a compare-and-despair moment.

- Choose to replace comparing and despairing with something that builds you up: pamper yourself, learn a new skill, work on a project or hobby that you are passionate about, or do something nice for someone else.

- Remember that there are approximately 400,000 types of flowers in the world. They are all beautiful in their own way. None of them are worrying about what the other flowers look like. They bloom and flourish on their own and together. Even weeds have some very beautiful blooms. They flourish just as bright because no one has told them they are weeds. As a matter of fact, you may even call them flowers, like the ox-eye daisy and the buttercup.

Calmfidence Killer #8:
Excessive Self-Consciousness

Being overly self-conscious can really throw you off balance. When you focus too much on yourself, it's really hard to focus on others and what's going on around you. It's easy to believe people are watching your every move, but then you realize they are watching *their* every move. People (with the exception of your family and close friends) really aren't that concerned about you. I chuckle here because I know that sounds terrible, but other people are pretty wrapped up in their own heads. Like you, they're thinking about themselves and all the things they are self-conscious of, or they're thinking about all the stuff going on in their own lives. When I first started working in front of the camera I can remember standing under the bright lights in the middle of a big television studio with all the cameras pointing at me. I felt so self-conscious in the beginning because all eyes were on me. Over time, I realized that everyone was concerned about their own job and getting it right. The lighting guy was looking for shadows, the camera operators were framing their shot, the makeup artist was checking her work, and the audio technician was checking the sound. Even though I was the subject they were working on, they were focused on their own needs. Now I stand there and let them do their jobs and don't even give it a second thought. As a matter of fact, I try to think of ways I can be helpful and informed about what they need. You can do this in pretty much any situation where you feel self-conscious. Start focusing on others' needs. Realize that they are just trying to get through their day as well as you are. Once you get out of your own head and start focusing on others, you forget about your worries for a little while. This kind of forgetfulness can be very liberating. It allows you to live in the present and respond in a genuine and natural way to the world around you. When we stop dwelling on ourselves, we begin to see our connections to each other and we are more alive. When your thoughts are "How can I help?" instead of "I hope they like me," the whole world changes.

How to turn around the Calmfidence killer of excessive self-consciousness:

* First, do what you can to feel like you've got your act together before you interact with others. Prepare, plan, work on your

calm and confidence using some of the techniques in this book, and do the best you can to show up strong (or good enough!) and then . . . forget about yourself.

- Get out of your own way by focusing on others. Adopt a service-oriented mindset of "How can I help?"

- Remember that everyone else is worrying about themselves and what they've got going on in their work and lives.

Calmfidence Killer #12: Self-Sabotage

Neglecting yourself and your health throws you off balance—and this will of course affect your ability to show up with your full potential in any situation. This includes not getting enough sleep, not exercising, overeating, drinking too much, taking drugs, allowing yourself to get overwhelmed with far too many to-dos, and so on. When you are run down, your body can't do its job correctly, and, because the body and mind are connected, you might then feel unmotivated and unable to handle the different or difficult situations that confront you. Tired and run-down bodies and minds have no stamina, no chutzpah. When we pay a lot of money for that new car, pair of designer shoes, or piece of jewelry, we go out of our way to take good care of these items and pro-tect our investments. We want them to stay sparkling and new. But our health, bodies, and minds are given to us free of charge, and we don't always protect them. We can't go out and buy new bodies when the used ones wear out. What if we treated our bodies and minds as if they were worth millions? After all, your body truly is priceless and irreplaceable. When you feel your best, you can expect the best—even demand the best—that life has to offer.

Recently I was having a conversation with a casting director at the training studio in New York City where I teach my group classes. The majority of the other teachers there are either casting directors or agents. Chatting with them before and after our classes gives me the wonderful opportunity to get some great insight into how their end of the business works and what they like and dislike about working with performers. I get to hear some pretty interesting stories.

This casting director shared a frustration with me that he said he has seen too many times: performers self-sabotaging themselves just before a big audition or meeting. He told me about a young woman who he thought had great potential. He helped her land a big audition. Then he found out that she went out and celebrated the night before by getting very drunk. She came to the audition hung over. She had low energy and was completely off her game. The audition didn't go well, and the client's first impression of her was so bad that it precluded her from consideration in any future projects as well. The casting director told me I would be surprised by just how often this happens. He believes this type of self-sabotage happens because of a lack of Calmfidence and too much self-doubt. In chapter 3, "Self-Care Calmfidence," we'll look at how you can manage and prevent this type of self-sabotage and take better care of yourself to really build up your calm and confidence.

How to turn around the Calmfidence killer of self-sabotage:

- Check in on how you are treating yourself. Are you being kind? Are you taking care of your mind, body, and spirit as if they were worth millions of dollars? If not, ask yourself why.

- Take special care before an important meeting or event. Establish an "A-Game" routine that helps you show up at your best.

- Celebrate after a big opportunity, not before.

- If you have doubts about your worthiness, make a list of all the reasons you have earned the right to show up with confidence. Sometimes we need to see things in writing to convince ourselves that we can go the distance and reach a goal.

- Always ask yourself, "Is what I'm about to do going to build me up, or tear me down?"

If you're thinking about all of your own Calmfidence killers right now, don't get discouraged. As I stated earlier, we've all got them; no one is immune. Just remember that you can have control over most of your Calmfidence killers. If it's a bad habit or a way of thinking that you've been doing for a long time, maybe even years, don't expect to turn it around immediately—that's not realistic. It's going to take some time. Just take one step in the right direction each day. The best part is when you start to catch yourself in the middle of a Calmfidence killer and you identify it. That's when you can say, "Stop! I'm going to think, do, or try something different this time!" Maybe you'll start by simply taking better care of yourself and being kinder to yourself, which brings us to our next chapter: "Self-Care Calmfidence."

Calmfidence Killer Reminders

- Many Calmfidence killers are created in our own minds. We are the ones who give them power, so we are the ones who can take away their power.

- Combat Calmfidence killers with your positivity, your light, your honesty, and your spirit.

- Focus on being true to yourself and less on what other people think.

A Client's Story

"She's an amazing chef, but she just doesn't come across confident on camera," the producer said over the phone. "The network really wants to give her a shot at her own cooking show but isn't sure we can get her to where we need her to be. Do you think you can help?"

I've worked with many experts and professionals who are great at what they do—until you put them on stage or in front of a television camera. When the spotlight gets turned on, so does their inner critic. When the stunning chef entered my training room, she conveyed a contagious passion for food. We talked and laughed, and she even made me salivate about the possibilities for lunch after the session. Then I put her in front of the camera and she became a different person—stiff, self-conscious, and unsure of herself.

"Who are you talking to?" I asked.

"My father," she said. "I always picture that I'm talking to my father when I talk to the camera."

Now, normally I recommend that my media clients aim to have a one-on-one conversation with a single viewer instead of envisioning themselves talking to a group or large audience of strangers—so her answer seemed in line. However . . .

Something's up, I said to myself. "Can you tell me a little bit about your father and your relationship with him?" I asked.

"Well, my father and I are very close, but he was angry when I decided to become a chef. He wanted me to become a doctor like him. I've been working hard to be successful so that I can prove to him that I made the right decision, but he's never satisfied with any of my achievements or even my TV segments."

This was it. The person she chose to talk to through that lens was not an ally, but a confidence-killing critic. Once we uncovered this we decided that from that moment on she would no longer picture her father watching her show, but instead speak to a viewer who really needed her help and enjoyed tuning in.

"I can't believe how much I enjoy being on camera now," she later told me. "Once I started picturing I was talking to a viewer through the camera who really needed my cooking advice and loved learning my recipes, everything changed." After that first training session, we worked for several weeks to break her habit of focusing on her father and instead picture a viewer who was an eager fan. Her improvement was drastic. The producers were thrilled, and she ended up getting her own national cooking show.

Calmfidence Killer Reflections

List three of your top Calmfidence killers:

_____

_____

_____

List one way that you think you could counteract each of your top three Calmfidence killers:

_____

_____

_____

3

Self-Care
Calmfidence

Self-care is giving the world the best of you,
instead of what's left of you.
Katie Reed

Self-care is one of the biggest daily Calmfidence builders we have. Yet, so many things can deplete our energy each day. Even when things are going pretty well, the normal everyday stress of balancing work and family life can take its toll. When we face challenges, our energy and sense of well-being can dwindle even more. Refilling your cup by taking care of your body, mind, and spirit is essential to creating more calm and confidence in your life every day. When we practice self-care, we are telling ourselves we are worth it. Self-care helps us to take responsibility for our own emotional, physical, psychological, and spiritual needs. When these four areas of our life are healthy and in an optimal state, we are at our best. When we practice consistent self-care habits, we handle stress better, which leads to more calm in our life. Positive self-care habits increase our confidence levels because we just feel better about ourselves and our abilities.

In chapter 2 I talked about the Calmfidence killer excessive self-consciousness and how one way to counteract it is by focusing on helping others. When it comes to self-care, this is where being self-focused is a positive strategy. You can't serve or help others without first serving yourself by taking care of your own needs and health. A study by the US

National Library of Medicine National Institute of Health showed that when medical students, who face high stress levels and workloads during medical school, committed to better self-care habits, they managed stress better, handled challenges with more confidence, and experienced an overall higher quality of life. Committing to better self-care will ultimately help them be better medical professionals who have more to give to serve others. I can tell you to eat better and exercise regularly, but you already know that those things are important. You just have to choose to do them if you really want to increase your calm and confidence. If you're like me, you probably fall on and off the wagon of eating healthy and getting your body moving. And that's okay too. Just know that when you have an important goal or event, or are going through a difficult time, those habits will help you handle everything better. Following are some other great ways you can practice self-care.

Go Behind the Scenes

Most of us are so overscheduled with work and home life that we rarely have down time. We wait for vacations or weekends to attempt to recharge our batteries. When we do have spare time, we fill it with distractions like movies, magazines, restaurants, drinks, hobbies, entertainment, and exercise. We focus on anything, and everything, except just peace and quiet.

Don't get me wrong here—all the things I just mentioned are important and enjoyable ways to spend time with people you care about, keep fit, and get pleasure from interests and hobbies you love. But down time spent alone and in quiet allows you to tap into places you simply can't reach and activate in any other way. Sure, you've probably had some great inspiration and insight during a run, a bike ride, a long walk in the woods, and even in the shower. But all of these things still involve doing "something," either physical or mental, and distractions are all around.

Many people are uncomfortable at the idea of completely stopping everything, being alone in silence, and being alone in their own minds. It can be downright scary for some people who find it hard to sit still for long and to remove themselves from everything else going on in their lives in order to be alone. But practicing quieting your mind and body in solitude can have a profound effect on every aspect of your life. Deep in the recesses of the human mind lie incredible intuition, discoveries, and intelligence that you can only tap into when you are quiet and alone with just your thoughts. Eyes closed, doors closed, just being in the moment inside yourself. Aha moments, the birth of new ideas, and answers and direction slowly rise to the surface when you truly give them a chance to emerge through inner peace and quiet.

Think about it. Behind the scenes is always where most of the magic happens. It's usually the stuff that the average person doesn't get to see that makes a great movie and creates the magic of television. It's the years of hard work and deep focus that suddenly make someone appear to be an "overnight success." A great book cannot be written without going behind the scenes and tapping into the *inside job*. Great inventions, new music, ideas, and goals all come from the *inside job*. I'm talking about meditation, and concentration of time spent looking inward instead of outward. Some people don't know how to meditate, and they think it takes too much time to light incense, cross their legs, and chant "Om." So, let's change the word *meditation* to *inside job*. You decide how you want to do it, where, and when. When you work on your *inside job*, you'll have an amazing, solid launching pad for any outside job you have to tackle. This is the only job in the world that gives you inner Calmfidence. It unlocks amazing abilities and talents. It taps into spirit, wisdom, encouragement, and fire.

You cannot wait until you have time to collect your thoughts or calm your mind, body, and spirit. You have to *make* time. In the same way we are told to prepare for storms ahead of time with emergency kits, we need to prepare our minds daily BEFORE a storm of life hits. If you wait until you need gas to fill your tank, you may run out.

Start with small doses. Close your eyes and take a few deep breaths. At first your mind will run wild. You'll have a thousand thoughts and feel like it isn't working. But just stick with it for two minutes, then five minutes, and increase the time gradually to as long as you want. Maybe that's ten minutes in the morning. Don't put pressure on yourself to expect immediate major progress. The more you practice relaxing and clearing your mind, the deeper you'll be able to go. Know and trust that even short sessions of silence will have a calming effect on your mind and body. Check out chapter 17, "Calmfidence Exercises," for some simple and easy ways to work a few fun and effective daily meditations into your life.

Make a Place for Calmfidence

It's important to have a place you can go to tune out the world and tune in to yourself. Create a retreat, a spot just for you that you can begin to associate with peace and calm. It should be a special place to unwind where you can settle, contemplate, and separate yourself from the daily grind. It can be an area of your home, a place where you can take a walk, even just a special chair you can sit in before your household wakes up in the morning. Be sure it's an effortless place that you can have access to anytime you want to be alone.

From late spring to early fall, I turn my front porch into a spot where I can write, think, have a cup of tea, or just close my eyes and listen to the birds and my wonderful wind chimes. You can do this on any size porch, deck, or patio. Fill it with flowers, plants, things you love, a table for your coffee or tea, a rocking chair, chimes, flags, hanging baskets, bird cages, candles, and pillows.

Your special space can be a section of your house or office—I use my home office as well. I decorated it in vintage Victorian décor, which I love, and I am surrounded by things that reflect who I am. I have an antique lounge, a Tiffany-style dragonfly lamp, incense, candles, pillows, a journal, notebooks, and a bookcase filled with books that have shaped and touched me. A client of mine who is Hindu has a mobile prayer set-up that she carries with her, along with incense, to create a place of peace, reflection, and prayer at work, a hotel, and anywhere else she finds herself in the world. Other clients connect to their peaceful place with sentimental stones, crystals, essential oils, flowing scarves, candles, collectables, and music.

Your place could even be a nearby grove or forest that feels sacred to you, a small pocket park in your city or town, or a mountain just outside of it. As author and psychologist Dr. Wayne Dyer always said, "Nature is therapy." Studies from Japan have shown that people who spend time in forests or among trees and bushes lower their levels of the stress hormone cortisol, slow their heart rates, and lower their blood pressure. The forest environment helps people feel livelier; it increases their concentration and even helps minimize symptoms of depression and ADHD. Plants and trees emit a substance called phytoncides that help to protect them from bugs and germs and also have a positive impact on human health. *Forest bathing*—immersing yourself in the green colors, sounds, and smells of the plants and trees in forests—creates higher activity of the parasympathetic nervous system, which promotes relaxation and reduces the sympathetic nerves associated with the fight-or-flight reaction to stress.

Good Night, Sleep Tight, for More Calm and Confidence

Sleep is at the foundation of self-care. According the National Library of Medicine, optimism and self-esteem are directly effect by the quality of your sleep. The sweet spot for a more confident day falls between six and eight hours of continuous sleep. Sleeping less than six hours or over nine hours has been associated with low self-esteem and low optimism. As research by the American Psychological Association shows, sleep allows our brain to recharge. When you recharge, you're able to feel more calm. People are just happier when they get the proper amount of sleep. Your body and mind need to fully rest, rejuvenate, and repair so that you can start a new day fresh and full of energy. Otherwise you will feel frazzled and overwhelmed. Here are some great ways you can get the zzz's you need:

- Aim to get to bed by 10 p.m. Falling off to sleep somewhere between 10 p.m. and 11 p.m. will ensure you get the length of sleep cycles you need, even if your schedule requires you to be an early riser. It's also much harder to fall asleep when you are overtired.

- Ask your doctor about calcium, magnesium, melatonin, GABA, and L-tryptophan. All have been shown to help with sleep.

- Let your mind flake—think of mundane and unimportant things like how you'd like to organize a closet in your home, what walls you'd like to repaint, flowers you'd like to plant, what shirt goes with what pants, or items in your home you'd like to donate. This works better than counting sheep and will keep you from thinking or worrying about more pressing issues that you can't do anything about while you're lying in bed anyway.

- Lighten up or play: read funny or light-hearted books or work on word search games, crossword puzzles or other games. Unwind and tap into calming creativity with adult coloring books. There are so many of these available today with different themes for everyone. Coloring helps to relax the fear center of your brain and reduces stress and anxiety.

- Visit chapter 16, "Natural Calmfidence Remedies," for things that can help you "get your calm on," like cherries, chamomile, lavender, and lemon balm extract.

- Milk it! Drinking warm milk before bed really can make you sleepy. It's another natural source of L-tryptophan!

- Journal; write down at least three things you are grateful for.

- Eat lightly and early; on those nights when sleep is most important, give your body a break from trying to digest a heavy meal while lying on your back.

- Avoid reading emails or checking in with social media right before bed or in the middle of the night; officially close shop for sleep! There are several reasons reading emails at these times will not serve you well. The light from your phone will wake up your brain—even if the brightness is turned down. When we read, the wheels of our mind start to turn, and our brain assumes it's time for action. Problems and worries seem worse in the middle of the night. Observing all the stuff going on in everyone else's life on social media can work for or against you, depending on your current situation and theirs. Last, the likelihood of reading something that might upset or worry you—or make you feel like you need to take action about a situation that you can't really take care of in the middle of the night—is very great. Don't set yourself up for stress or worry at night; whatever it is can wait until morning, when you can really do something about it.

- Limit alcohol; a little alcohol may relax you and get you sleepy, but if you have a few drinks you'll most likely wake up when the alcohol starts to wear off, about two hours later. Several years ago, I met exercise and fitness legend Jack LaLanne at a medical media awards dinner. I asked him what his secret to living a long healthy life was. He told me, "Eating right and getting plenty of exercise." Not surprising. I asked him if he drank alcohol. He said, "Only one glass of red wine a night, but never two." I've tried to stick to this (which is not always easy), and when I do, I sleep like a baby. When I don't, I have broken sleep, wake up before I complete a sleep cycle (a cycle is three hours), and don't feel well rested when I wake up in the morning.

- Tune Out. Watching late-night TV, especially dark, disturbing, agitating, overly emotional programming, is like digital caffeine: it will put your brain into high gear. For more than a decade, I hosted a show called *Education Showcase* at the CNBC studios that was sponsored by CNBC and Discovery Communications. It was an interview show where we talked about all the educational programming you could find on television. Executives from the PBS Kids channel Sprout were guests on one of our episodes, and during our interview they described why the channel's nighttime programming was so different from the daytime lineup. The channel had conducted a great deal of research about children's sleep/wake cycles and found that evening programming needed to be slower, with less quick-moving imagery; have more muted colors and brightness; and contain soothing music so that children would not get overstimulated leading up to bedtime. The same is true for adults. Television stimulates our brains, senses, and emotions. When we watch too late, we are "tuned" up, not winding down on our way to a calm slumber.

- Exercise is wonderful and necessary, but it energizes you. Do it too close to bedtime and you will be invigorated instead of sleepy. If you can only work out at night, know that you'll need a couple of hours to settle down before you can expect to get sleepy.

- Avoid caffeine and sugar late in the day—this is the dynamic duo of hyperactivity, as they both kick your body and brain into turbo drive. You might be able to get away with them at dinner if you eat at 6 p.m. But maybe not, depending on your individual reaction. Why take a chance at a time when you need a good night of sleep? Save it for the morning.

- Try not to fall asleep on the couch or in a room other than your bedroom. When you do wake up in the middle of the night or sooner—and you will since you are not in your normal comfy bed—you'll have to drag yourself into your bed and will wake up more just trying to get there. You will have wasted your seduction into a deep sleep that might have lasted hours longer if it happened in your bed.

- Try to avoid any type of conflict or argument right before bed or difficult conversation at a time when you should be winding things down. Obviously, we don't always have control over this, but many times we do. Choose to address what you can before the approaching bedtime.

- Try not to review tomorrow's to-do list in your head. Instead, recap the things you are happy you did during the day, your accomplishments, and so on, and feel satisfied about ending another productive day. Even if you didn't get everything done or there's more to do tomorrow, write it down on paper or your device, download it out of your head, and put it aside knowing that you can follow tomorrow's plan of action—tomorrow!

- Think about future events that are pleasant, hopeful, and something you are looking forward to, or something positive you'd like to achieve. Don't lie there in dread thinking about future things you are concerned about; there's nothing you can do about them right now anyway, and they will only keep you awake.

- Try to get yourself ready for the next day before you lie down in bed. Select your clothes, make lunch, get things ready for your kids if you have children, organize paperwork, fill up your car's gas tank (or charge your car's battery), and so on. Plan ahead and get as much done before getting in to bed as possible.

A Calming Sleep Exercise

Turn yourself off with the "light-bulb moment" exercise—this visualization exercise works! First, get in the most comfortable position you can. Now picture bright light bulbs placed on your body, starting at your toes. See them on top of your foot, on your heel and ankle, and on each toe. Next, place more light bulbs onto your shins, knees, thighs, hips, navel, chest, back, and shoulders. Now do the same with your fingers, palms, wrists, elbows, and shoulders. Finish off with your neck, chin, nose, cheeks, eyes, ears, and finally the top of your head. Now slowly and deliberately start back at your toes and turn off each light. As you see each light go dark, feel each area relax. Then move on to the next. By the time you get to the top of your head, you will either fall asleep or have a much more relaxed body and mind.

When you take better care of yourself, you have the energy and vitality you need to take control of each day. You can pace yourself, manage your emotions better, increase your sense of well-being, and experience more optimism. Self-care is important every day, but it is paramount during challenging times when major life events, big disappointments, and storms come our way. Which leads us to part 2 of this book, "Resilient Calmfidence."

A Client's Story

"I wake up with knots in my stomach most days. I totally blanked out during a meeting at work last week. Between you and me, I'm exhausted, and I feel like I've lost my confidence," said Kate, a senior vice president for a national beauty brand. Even though she was smart and super successful, she was struggling with her confidence daily. She had worked with the same team for five years until a new division opened up, and now she was in charge of a completely new team, reporting to a new boss. Long hours, little sleep, new personalities, new procedures, and new quotas had Kate doubting herself big time. Work was no longer her comfort zone. Her inner critic was hijacking her self-talk and her self-esteem. It started affecting the way she was interacting with her coworkers, and Kate was not the easiest person to get along with these days. She was burning herself out and doing nothing to build herself back up again.

I met Kate when the company hired me to work with the team on interpersonal skills, communication skills, and my signature Calmfidence strategies. Kate felt she had no time for this and chose not to attend any of the group sessions. But her boss insisted that she make time for a few one-on-one private sessions. When Kate rushed into the small conference room where I was set up, she was agitated and distracted.

"Can we get this over with as soon as possible? I've got a ton of work I need to take care of," she said.

I smiled and asked, "What else do you need to take care of these days, Kate?"

She stopped mid-stride and looked at me with a confused expression. I asked, "Are you taking care of *yourself*, Kate?" She sat down and stared at me. Then she looked around the windowless room and started to cry.

Kate and I worked out a daily Calmfidence plan that had her start each day waking up to a sound machine that played a wind-chimes alarm that she loved. This way she could keep her phone charging in another room and resist the urge to look at it first thing. Instead of feeling instantly bombarded by email, scrolling through social media, or looking at the bad news of the day, Kate now headed right to the small sitting room she had filled with objects that brought her calm and joy. She got up just fifteen minutes earlier and began her day in silence and gratitude and then pictured the day ahead as she'd like things to unfold in a positive way. She started scheduling in a walk either at lunch or later in the evening, and herbal tea replaced wine during the week. Kate created a more peaceful bedroom—no TV, and a bowl of lavender buds and uplifting books on her nightstand. The last thing she would do before falling asleep was to recap her day in her thoughts with what went right that day instead of what went wrong.

Although many of these changes are small and simple, they had a profound impact on Kate and they affected who she was when she showed up at the office. She felt less over-whelmed and more able to communicate with her coworkers in a relaxed manner. "Here's to a successful first quarter with the new team!" Kate's boss said and smiled as she raised her glass a few months later. Kate was surrounded her coworkers, who now felt more like friends. Once Kate started changing the way she began and ended each day, she also began to change the stories she was telling herself.

"I have such a sense of well-being now. I feel good about myself. I have more energy but I'm calm at the same time. Even when the pressure is on, I just seem to handle it better. I'm able to say *I've got this* more often," Kate told me.

Calmfidence Reflections

List three things you could do each day to improve self-care and feel more Calmfidence:

_____

_____

_____

List three places you could go or spaces you could create for quiet and calm:

_____

_____

_____

Part Two

Resilient Calmfidence

4

Calmfidence
Setbacks

Don't quit. Never give up trying to build the world you
see, even if others can't see it. Listen to your drum and your
drum only. It's the one that makes the sweetest sound.

Simon Sinek

It was the spring of 2020 in New York, and I was right in the heart of
the worst outbreak of COVID-19 in the United States. All I could
think about was survival—toilet paper, Lysol, Clorox wipes, our stock
of food and medicine, keeping my elderly mother safe, and trying to
keep a sixteen-year-old with a new driver's license in the house. Many
people were talking about all the lofty things they might try to accomplish during quarantine, like writing a book, but I actually had to. I had
signed the publishing contract for this book on January 15, 2020, one
of the most exciting days of my life. I achieved a goal I had been working on for over ten years. I was finally going to be a published author.
But I couldn't concentrate. I didn't write a word during the spring of
2020. Not . . . one . . . word. I realized I just had to let go. I reached
out to a dear friend of mine who is a psychologist for a phone session
and a reality check. He helped me get some perspective and cut myself
some slack. I didn't beat myself up about it. I had to trust that the words
would come again once things settled down a bit—and by June and
July, they did. I emerged from that first quarantine with a new outlook

on what was important in life and new insights on finding personal calm when the world around you is in chaos. Once again I relearned that we grow the most when we are challenged.

When you get thrown off your game, go through a life change, experience a disappointment, or have something crazy and unexpected happen in your life, like a global pandemic, your Calmfidence can get shaken for sure. When you're dazed and confused, it's not a good time to take action. You can't think clearly. A global pandemic and war are probably the most extreme examples, but personal setbacks of any level can have a negative impact on us at any time in our lives. But the wisdom, compassion, and strength of Calmfidence can spring from the broken places and cracks in our life's path and build your resilience.

Retreat So You Can Emerge with Force

You've heard the old saying about getting right back on the horse after a fall; this is good advice to help you stay persistent. But some setbacks are bigger and harder and can't be brushed off immediately. Sometimes we need to fall apart and regroup so that we can come back in a way that builds our resilience and makes us even stronger. You may need to retreat, so you can emerge with force. Knowing when you need to pull back and cut yourself some slack is very empowering. Doing nothing IS doing something. Give yourself permission to rest, reassess, and recharge your batteries. Inner strength comes from a well of calm, quiet, contemplative stillness. When you are empty, exhausted, beaten up, or filled with sorrow, take time for yourself to just be. Then you can go back to the well to fill up your cup again. This could mean staying in your PJ's all day and eating a half-gallon of ice cream, going on a long hike in the hills to have a good cry, binge-watching a show, taking a few personal days off from work, or getting out for a change of scenery to clear your head and break a negative cycle. It may be about accepting the fact that time really is the only thing that heals. It may even mean seeking the help of a professional to deal with your emotions. Give yourself a time frame on your retreat. Once the dust settles, once you catch your breath and begin to think straight again, you can go into recovery mode.

R-E-C-O-V-E-R-Y Mode

Get into *R-E-C-O-V-E-R-Y mode* to increase your resilience. The initial R in *recovery* stands for *redirecting* your thoughts. Kick-start your brain back into a positive direction. Although you may not feel like it, make a list of what is right in your life; what you are thankful for, like your health, family, and friends. Add to the list every day. Look at the list when you wake up in the morning and when you go to bed at night.

The first E in recovery mode stands for *evaluate* the situation from another perspective. Could it have been worse? Is there any good at all that could come from it? Are there people in worse situations right now than you are? Do you have any different options in the way you can respond to the situation?

The C in recovery mode stands for *connect* with people who support you and believe in you and your abilities. Communicate with them.

The O in recovery mode stands for *open*. Open your mind to looking at fresh and different options. Ask the people who believe in you what new possibilities they see for you. The truism "When one door closes, another opens" has been around a long time. Look for that new open door.

The V in recovery mode stands for *value*. No matter what happens to you, you are of great value; everyone is. There are people who also greatly value you right now and you may not even realize it.

The next E in recovery mode stands for *embrace* where you are right now. We grow the most when we're challenged and tested, and when we go through tough times and change.

The next R in recovery mode stands for *realize* that this too will pass. Nothing lasts forever. There will be a day in the future where you look back from a very different place.

And finally, the Y in recovery mode stands for *yell*. Vent if you have to. Open the window and scream out loud. Get it out. Don't hold in your anger, your sorrow, or your disappointment. Once you let it out, it's so much easier to move on.

Take a Break from Happiness

"What makes you think you are supposed to be happy all the time?" asked my dear friend and mentor, psychologist Dr. Thomas Nardi.

"Isn't that what we are all supposed to be aiming for? Doesn't everyone want to be happy?" I said.

"It's not realistic. It's okay to just be in neutral. Neither happy or sad," he replied. This was a turning point for me. It was actually a relief. So much emphasis is placed on being happy in our society that the constant pursuit of happiness can be exhausting. We can get down on ourselves because we think we should be happier than we are. Trying so hard to be happy can make us unhappy!

- Don't expect to be happy all the time.
- When you've experienced a setback, sit with your disappointment, sorrow, anxiety, stress, or fear—fully experience it, don't fight it, don't feel shame, don't judge your emotions. Let them flow. Work through them. You can't force the process. You can't force grieving.
- It's okay to not be okay.
- Riding along in neutral is normal and good before you get to the next time where you experience happiness.
- Create space to live your emotions. It's cathartic to put on a sad movie, listen to affecting music, or sift through old photos to allow for a release of emotions—to let it all out.
- Reach out to others to see how they have handled similar experiences.
- Practice self-care. When you are down, it is not the time to run yourself down even further.

Work Through Your Fears

Don't wait until you no longer feel afraid. Recognizing that you are afraid *only* means you are afraid. It does not mean you must postpone living or doing the thing that you fear. Other than in the case of a pandemic or health-related setback, admit that you are afraid—and then act in spite of the fear. The more you *do*, the less the fear will win out and the more grit and resilience you will have. For instance, if you bombed that speech or big interview last time, it's natural that you'll fear it might happen again. But that's all in your head—your body feels the fear, but the source is in your mind. Your thoughts create your emotions. Your current fear is created and maintained by your beliefs. If you're afraid, it's probably because you're saying things to yourself like, "I'm going to fail. What if I look foolish?" Challenge your thoughts. There is no evidence that you will fail or look foolish this time, and no proof it would be horrible if you did.

Read the signs of your body—what you are reading in your body as fear is no more than the adrenaline flowing. When you feel that adrenaline, remind yourself that it is your body preparing for action. Label it as energy. It's up to you to determine how you label it, and the way you label it is how you are going to feel.

Learn to Say "So What"

One thing that most of us are really good at is being hard on ourselves. We just have to get better at saying *so what* every now and then. This doesn't mean you stop caring about important things, responsibilities, or consequences. It just means caring less about what people think and allowing yourself to make mistakes, to be human, to have flaws. Saying *so what* opens doors to *next time*. So what if things didn't go well this time? So what if things didn't work? *So what* can help you get out of your own way and get onto the road to *next time*, when things could (and quite likely will) go better.

A Different Angle

In my career, it seems I've always found my way in through the back door, the window, or a hole in the roof, or I've created a door where there wasn't one, usually after trying the traditional route and failing. I've found this to be the case for my most successful clients as well. Just because you tried one way to make something happen and it didn't, doesn't mean it's over. There is never just one right way to do anything. Coming at things from different angles means you have to work a little harder, change your perspective, and not take no for an answer. Sometimes the universe puts brick walls in front of you to see just how bad you really want something.

There are people who get discouraged by roadblocks and people who get fired up to get around them or over them. You can choose how to react. We don't always value the things that come easy, anyway. The more you approach challenges from different angles, the more you build resilience.

Perform PRR

After a setback you can perform a type of personal P-R-R: personal responsibility resuscitation. Ask yourself:

* What can I do to get back on my feet?
* Will I let this conquer me, or will it strengthen me?
* What can I do differently next time?
* What can I do to be more prepared next time?
* What baby steps can I take right now?
* How can I be in more control of the situation?
* What other angle or perspective can I approach this from?
* What did I learn? What do I need to learn and where can I learn it?
* What did I learn from my experience that could help other people?
* How am I stronger after getting through this?

Get Out of Your Head—Volunteer Instead

In chapter 2, "Calmfidence Killers," we talked about excessive self-consciousness and getting out of your head. Volunteering helps us get outside of our own woes. Many studies show that volunteering leads to better health and happiness, regardless of socioeconomic status. When we take the focus off our own troubles and problems, we unblock our own stagnant mucky pond and get the clean waters running again. Volunteering also can help remind us that we are part of a bigger picture, one where we can relate to each other, share our stories, and even find reassuring common ground. When you are there to help and be of service, it's like a vacation from your own worries.

Something Better

We can prepare, plan, and take full responsibility for our thoughts and actions, and our life can still crash and burn. It may be because there is something better in store. People get fired or laid off from jobs only to be thankful later because they ended up finding a job where they were happier. A breakup with a lover or spouse can seem like the end of the world until you meet your real soul mate later.

The home my husband and I had our hearts set on buying fell through at the last minute, but we ended up in a home we still live in today—one that we love even more, and which is closer to family and friends in a wonderful neighborhood. We suffered from heartbreaking infertility trying to start a family, and every time a pregnancy attempt fell through it was devastating. Then we were finally blessed with our son. He was the one we were supposed to have. Any of those previous egg/sperm combinations would not have resulted in the combination that created who he is. Maybe the setback you had or are having right now is really setting you up for something better. That possibility is always on my mind now.

Just a Crummy Day Calmfidence

Okay, so you feel down today. Nothing is going your way. You're in a terrible mood and not really sure why. It almost feels good to wallow in it for a while. And here's the critical self-care key: don't fight it. Don't try to justify it. Don't beat yourself up about it. Just live it for right now. This too will pass.

It's a good time to pull back if you can and partake in some alone time if possible. Sometimes just a ten-minute break behind closed doors can make all the difference. If this mood continues and you've had your fill of it, here are some tips to help you snap out of it:

* Crank your favorite song. You know, that one you've adopted as your personal anthem that flips an internal switch in you every time you hear it.

* Call an old friend—someone who will listen to you rant for just a little while and then say something stupid or sarcastic to help you get over yourself.

- Make a mental list of at least five things that you're thankful for in your life. Health? A safe home? A pet? A good meal? Older loved ones still alive? A good neighbor or friend? Children, spouse, family members? Freedom? Once you start, it's amazing how you'll find more than five quickly.

- Remind yourself that how you feel about things is a choice. You choose how you react to things; you choose how you view things, and you choose to be happy or not.

- Get moving. Go for a walk or run. Wander around your favorite store for a while. Go for a drive (with that song blasting) or do something nice for someone else.

- Play. Do anything that makes you feel like a child again. Swing on a swing, play tic-tac-toe, play a video game, play a board game with your kids, play hide-and-seek.

- Laugh. Put on your favorite comedy, tune in to a comedy channel on cable or satellite radio, or visit a joke website. Laughter can have a positive effect on the health of your mind and body, so it can definitely help you during a crummy day!

- Pamper yourself. Take a bath, get a massage or facial, take a mental health day, or just collapse in a chair for a while. Remember, sometimes you have to retreat so that you can emerge again with force. On a crummy day, give yourself whatever mini or maxi retreat you can. It will give you a chance to recharge your batteries and regain Calmfidence.

Accept that this is just an off day. Know that tomorrow will be a fresh, clean slate.

Say Goodbye

One of my clients had a terrible fear of public speaking and extreme performance anxiety. It finally came out that she had had a very hurtful public experience years earlier, when she was young. During a performance on stage at a competitive international event, she had stuttered and stumbled and could not hide her embarrassment and shyness. Her competition was more than happy to take advantage of it, and the audience and her community actually taunted her and shamed her live on stage and after the event as well. She felt personally defeated and was made to feel that she had let her whole country down. Shortly afterward, she moved to the United States and avoided the spotlight, but she had carried this experience with her for twenty-five years, reliving it over and over again. She came to me because she had been offered an opportunity to appear on television once again in her home country. She wanted to prepare, so she scheduled a coaching session with me.

When I put her in front of the camera for media training, as soon as she tried to speak, her fear shut her down. I tried everything I could think of to get her to relax during our first few sessions and, after she finally told me her story, I concluded that she had a genuine mental block. My goal now was to help this client understand that she was no longer the same person she was seeing in her mind from so long ago. She was now an adult with a wealth of life experience, a strong sense of self, and emotional maturity. She was going to have to say goodbye to that young girl from her past.

Her homework was to meditate on that past event. To go back in time in her mind's eye to see the young girl as she was, to look her in the eye and verbally say goodbye. She practiced this day and night for one week. The difference in our next session was remarkable. It wasn't a complete turnaround, but she had made vast progress as she committed to visualizing and meditating and making this goodbye as real as she could. The little girl had been with her as a companion for so long and it was going to take time to get this squatter out of her mind, but the eviction notice was finally being served loud and clear.

This client's experience reminded me of a difficult time I went through in college when my parents sold my childhood home and moved to New Hampshire. I thought I was so independent and all grown up, but I couldn't seem to get past the loss. One of my psychology teachers at the time told me about a technique of saying goodbye. He suggested that I physically park in front of my old house and get out and say goodbye to it. It sounded weird to me at the time, but I did it. It felt silly. I did it anyway. I can tell you, it really did make a remarkable difference.

What baggage are you carrying around? What setbacks have you let take root in your subconscious? Don't let them become like space-junk floating around in your mental atmosphere. Call them back and speak out loud to them—and say goodbye once and for all.

It takes courage to let go of the past. It takes courage to say goodbye to who we used to be and become who we are meant to be. Which leads us to our next chapter: "Courageous Calmfidence."

Find Your Calm During Setbacks

When you experience a setback, find your calm by doing the following:

- Retreating: take a step back, regroup, cut yourself some slack.
- Letting go of the pressure to be happy. Let neutral be okay.
- Aiming for a *so what* attitude for a while to let things roll off your back a bit.
- Letting go of past stress.

Find your confidence during setbacks by:

- Getting into R-E-C-O-V-E-R-Y mode: redirect, evaluate, connect, open your mind, communicate your needs, value yourself, embrace where you are, realize this will pass, yell if you have to.
- Taking a different approach. Take a risk to try a new way.
- Working through your fears. Confidence is always found when you face your fears head on.
- Accepting that setbacks and challenges build resilience and toughness.

Calmfidence Reflections

List three ways you can retreat so you can recharge:

_____

_____

_____

List three ways you can get into R-E-C-O-V-E-R-Y mode:

_____

_____

_____

List three different ways you could approach a challenge you are facing:

_____

_____

_____

5

Courageous Calmfidence

Life is a daring adventure or nothing at all.

Helen Keller

I was conducting my TV Host Connection Weekend in New York City, a two-day training program for aspiring and working broadcast talent who have an idea for a new TV show concept that they would like to pitch and host. Throughout the weekend I would help them flesh out their ideas and build their confidence in front of the camera, and on the final day they would present to the camera while a panel of casting directors and talent agents viewed them on a large TV screen. Amber, a dog lover who worked at a busy animal shelter in Virginia, was visiting New York for the first time and traveling alone. Soft-spoken but well-liked by the group, she was uncomfortable attending the event. Amber's show concept was to spotlight older dogs throughout the country who get overlooked for adoption and ultimately euthanized. It was remarkable to see the difference in Amber's personality when she talked about saving these dogs. She was no longer quiet, but enthusiastic and passionate as she advocated for animals who could not speak for themselves. But otherwise Amber was shy and overwhelmed, sitting between the current Miss America and a contributor from a CNN legal program. As the panel of talent agents and casting directors entered the room on the final day, a look of panic came over Amber's face and she ran out of the room.

I excused myself and found Amber in the hallway, her eyes filled with tears. "Amber, are you okay?" I asked. She replied, "I can't do this! I can't stand up there in front of that panel and talk. My heart is pounding!"

"Why did you come here? Do you want to be a TV star?" I asked.

"Why, no, not at all! I just want to help these dogs. I can't stand to think that these wonderful loving dogs are just waiting to die and no one really even knows their story and that they need a home," she replied.

"Then focus only on that," I said. "When you go back into the room for your turn in front of the camera, forget that the panel or anyone else in the room is even there. Picture yourself as if you are already live on the air, hosting your show and talking to people who want to adopt and save these dogs. Tell them about the wonderful personalities of the dogs and why they will make a great addition to their family."

Amber reentered the room on a mission. The look of determination on her face and the passionate energy she mustered up was really amazing. You could see that all of the other participants were rooting for her. She did a great job. Her presentation was powerful and uplifting. She was contagiously motivating. I think everyone in the room that day would have adopted a dog at that moment given the chance. Amber found her courage and passion in her purpose.

Getting Comfortable with Feeling Uncomfortable Builds Your Courage

It seems counterintuitive, but the discomfort of doing something new is often the very thing that can increase your courageous Calmfidence. Courage is not the absence of fear; it is action in the presence of fear. Deciding that you want something more than you are afraid of it can change everything. Learning to have more Calmfidence when you are uncomfortable and expanding your view of yourself and what you are capable of can change your world. Learning to get comfortable with being uncomfortable while reaching for your goals is worth its weight in gold.

On-a-Mission Calmfidence

A person on a mission has a goal, a direction, a plan, and a focus. Everybody loves the energy of a person who is going places, someone who is filled with passion, determination, and purpose. What a courageous adventure life could be if we looked at our time here on earth as being on a mission or following our calling. So many people sadly go through the motions, wander through life, or just feel like they don't have a specific purpose. But the happiest people I've ever met have viewed their life, their work, or their family as a mission or calling.

Maybe your calling is to raise amazing children who will contribute great things to our world and help other people. Maybe your calling is to help others enjoy their day at work. Maybe your calling is to use your skills to empower others in some way.

Whatever you do, if you start to look at it as your calling or mission, wonderful changes are headed your way. Think of your goal as your mission and calling. You will pursue it in a much different way. When I work with people who are experiencing the "impostor syndrome," one of the first things I'll say to them is, "Maybe you found your calling." Suddenly the look on their face changes as they consider the possibility.

Every expert was once a beginner. Every great artist, inventor, or philosopher was once a beginner. We are given the seeds of passion for something for a reason. If we do not courageously work through the fear, the doubt, the growing pains, the impostor syndrome, those seeds will never grow. And that would not only be sad for us, it would be sad for the world that could have benefited in some way from our time here. Life is a daring adventure or nothing at all.

Larger-Purpose Calmfidence

When you feel fear, ask yourself, "What is my purpose here?" Is it completely self-serving, or is your goal something that can bring value to others? Is there a way that your goal can be viewed in such a way that you can see you are being of service to others? When we work through fear knowing that our *why* is bigger than we are, it can help us get out of our own way. Are you advocating for others who do not have a voice or the platform to be heard like you do? Perhaps you are educating, informing, inspiring, or even entertaining others. All of these things serve other people's needs and can enrich their lives. When you feel fear, stress, or anxiety, try to take the focus off of yourself and concentrate on the result you are working toward.

Unique Calmfidence

There is no one in the world like you. It is truly incredible that we each have our own set of fingerprints. It's your personal code that proves you are unique. This means that when your hand touches this life, it's never been done in just that way by anyone else before. Everything you do is marked with your own personal energy. Just because others have done something before, it has never been done *your* way before, with your unique life force. And it will never again be done in the same way by anyone else. I tell this to my students and clients all the time: *Put your personal stamp on all that you do, during job interviews, performances, and all daily communications.*

MacGyver Calmfidence

MacGyver was a popular action/adventure television show from the late 1980s through the early 1990s. The main character, Angus MacGyver, was part secret agent, part handyman, and part mad scientist who could improvise solutions with everyday objects. The Urban Dictionary definition of a MacGyver is "someone who can jump-start a truck with a cactus." My own dad was a MacGyver who taught me how to mold glass with a blowtorch, create metal sculptures, build a deck, change a tire, and shoot a .357 magnum. Together we made a 3D suitcase-size cross-section of a house for science class to show the layers of walls—sheet rock, insulation, and plywood. The seventh-grade boys thought I was so cool.

My dad taught me how to improvise and figure stuff out on the fly, working with whatever I already had. When you trust that you can come up with solutions, you have Calmfidence in your abilities to say yes first, and then figure out later how to pull something off. Thanks to Dad's training, I've successfully done this many times throughout my life and career, helping friends in difficult situations and stepping up to the plate to get things done. When I decided I wanted to start my own business, I just kept saying yes when someone would ask, "Do you do interview skills training? Teleprompter training, media interview training, or public-speaking training?" I'd say "Yes, absolutely," and then I'd go figure out whatever additional knowledge I needed to learn, or find the resources I needed to get the training done to fit the clients' needs. It's amazing how much you can learn and how quickly you can learn it when you have to live up to your promises.

Trusting in yourself to believe that you can use your brain, your experience, and your ingenuity to figure things out is a gift you give to yourself. It was originally a gift I got from my dad, and I'm now passing it on to my son.

The Calmfidence Impostor

Many of my clients feel like impostors when they accept a request to be a speaker at an event or meeting, or are invited to appear on television as a guest expert or contributor. Often the first thought that goes through their mind is, *Surely there is someone else who knows more about this topic than me!* Or when they book that first job as an actor or TV or video host, they secretly worry that the person who hired them made a mistake and will find out they are really not that good.

Performers, authors, athletes, famous people, and professionals in every industry experience the impostor syndrome at some point. Of course there is probably someone else in the world who is more knowledgeable, has more experience, and more talent, but if you've been given a shot at a job, been asked to give your own personal expert opinion, or share your knowledge with an audience—you, my friend *are* the expert of the moment. This is when your courageous self-talk needs to kick in.

Tell yourself that you are good enough. You would not have been invited to speak unless someone else thought you belonged there. Maybe you were raised to not toot your own horn or you are simply modest, but if someone is looking to you as the expert, you've got to courageously own that role. Minimizing yourself, your knowledge, and your accomplishments helps no one. Sharing what you have learned, your achievements and success, *can* help others. Be the expert in your arena, your community, and your part of the universe. The other experts out there haven't been invited to the same party that you have been invited to. Can you imagine refusing to eat your next meal unless the world's greatest chef cooked it? Of course, that sounds silly. So own your expertise courageously. Give yourself permission to know that you have something unique to offer that cannot be found anywhere else.

Changing Calmfidence

One of the most inevitable things in life that we need to be courageous about is change. Life is change. But we often fear change. It makes us uncomfortable. We get set in our ways. We fixate on the "way things should be" or the "way they used to be." We don't take chances; we hold on to things longer than we should. Fearing change prevents us from living courageously. Growth cannot happen without change. They're called "growing pains" for a reason. They are uncomfortable and can even hurt. We cannot become someone better or stronger, or evolve in any way, without change. So instead of seeking ways to avoid change, if we can get in the habit of welcoming change, expecting change, and even deliberately creating change, we will be on our way to living with courageous Calmfidence. Courageous Calmfidence is not about a sure thing or a certainty—it's about trusting that you can and will handle anything that comes your way. It's not absolute Calmfidence. It's *enough* Calmfidence. And that's all you really need.

Calmfidence Alone

When I left my full-time job to go into my own business, it was a little nerve-wracking, not only because I was hoping I could make it on my own but because it was at times uncomfortable to be alone. I had always worked with groups of people, had someone to eat lunch with, joke around with, and a group to feel a part of. When I found myself going it alone, I felt naked. I had to get used to calling on clients alone, traveling alone, and eating meals at a table by myself surrounded by pairs or groups of other people. At first, I was self-conscious; it felt awkward. The more I did it, though, the easier it got. Now I travel all over the country and even internationally alone, and I can say that I am comfortable just about any place I go.

For otherwise surefooted people who don't normally venture out on their own, the thought of doing so can unnerve them. Odds have it that at some point you'll be in a situation where you'll have to go it alone whether you like it or not. No family, no kids, no friends or coworkers. So, experiment in advance and it won't throw you off so much when it does happen.

Eat in a diner, coffee shop, or restaurant alone even if it scares the heck out of you. Start at a counter first. Many times, the people who sit at the counter are alone too, so you'll be in good company and can experiment with striking up a conversation with other people around you. Immediately ask for the server's name or read their name tag and use their name. Establishing rapport with the server or host will increase your comfort level immediately. Work to develop the gift of gab and an interest in other people.

Courageous Calmfidence develops over time. But we can decide to be a bit more courageous each day. Throughout time, humans have found ways to create tools that help them do the heavy lifting, achieve things that they normally would not have been able to do, and get results faster than before. So it is with building your courage. There are tools you can use to help you find your Courageous Calmfidence, especially during stressful, challenging times when you might find yourself on shaky ground. Which brings us to our next chapter: "Calmfidence Tools."

Courageous Calmfidence helps boost your calm by:

- Learning to get comfortable feeling uncomfortable.
- Accepting and embracing change.

Courageous Calmfidence helps boost your confidence by:

- Knowing you don't need absolute confidence, you need just enough to take action.
- Being self-sufficient, trusting yourself when it's you and you alone.
- Embracing your uniqueness.
- Giving you a sense of purpose.

Calmfidence Reflections

List three things you could take action on even though you are afraid:

_____

_____

_____

List three things you'd like to get comfortable being uncomfortable with:

_____

_____

_____

List three unique things you have to offer:

_____

_____

_____

List three good things that have happened because something changed:

_____

_____

_____

List three things that could be your mission or calling:

_____

_____

_____

List three ways you can feel more Calmfidence when you are alone:

_____

_____

_____

6

Calmfidence Tools

We shape our tools and thereafter they shape us.

John M. Culkin

Throughout history, tools have helped humans function better. There are tools that increase our power, help us hold things together, help us create, keep things sharp, and even help us to see better. No matter how calm and confident we are, we all enter periods of walking on shaky ground, which threatens our Calmfidence. We need tools to help us hold ourselves together, help us create the life we want, build our resilience, and help us to see things more clearly. You can create your own Calmfidence tools that you can stockpile into an arsenal to keep up your sleeve for those moments when you find yourself on shaky ground. Tangible tools and mindset tools can help you get your act together, inspire you, prepare you, change your perspective, and help you remember your worth. These tools can help bring your mojo back and help you overrule your inner critic and conquer your doubts and fears. Here are a number of tools I use with my clients and myself. They might not all resonate with you. Try them on for size and feel free to morph them to fit your needs or inspire you to create some of your own.

Your Calmfidence Credit Card

Calmfidence is like cash; it's not always readily available when you need it! So, what do you do when you're short on cash while walking on that shaky ground? Whip out your credit card! You can create a Calmfidence "credit card" to carry in your wallet. On it write affirmations, successes, and even positive comments you've received from others. These are positive reminders to yourself of what you want and where you want to be.

- Include a few bullet points that list your strong points—things you know you are good at.
- Write a list of the things you are grateful for.
- Write down goals and dreams so they stay fresh and in sight.
- Laminate your card. Make it feel like a real credit card, thick and substantial. This will also make it last longer in your wallet.
- Charge up a storm. Use your Calmfidence credit card all the time, even when you think you don't need to use it—take a quick glance for a little extra special boost.
- Remember that repetition is the key. You need to repeat the Calmfidence messages in order to replace that old negative record in your brain.
- Update your card as new successes come your way.
- This is the kind of credit you want to build—it will build YOU up! And it really pays.

This Calmfidence credit card also happens to be a credibility card. So many of the people I work with deal with the impostor syndrome. No matter how long they've been doing what they've been doing, somehow they still feel like they are not really an expert or pro in their field. They brush off past success as being lucky or they minimize the depth of their experience, and many times they even forget just how much they've really done over the years.

A client of mine who has been a successful TV executive for several years really struggled with this. When I first told her to create her Calmfidence credit card she had a hard time coming up with stuff to put on it—until I gave her an assignment to do a brain dump on paper of all the things she had accomplished at work and in her personal life. Everything was fair game. Nothing was too small or insignificant. Eventually she filled up five pages of notes—and she couldn't believe her eyes! When I reviewed the list, it was amazing to me that so many of the small or insignificant things she listed were really a huge deal to just about anyone else who would read them. From those five pages we were able to come up with three different Calmfidence credit cards, credibility cards that apply to different challenges in her work and life. Till this day she still keeps them all in her wallet. This also helped her create an amazing résumé.

The Calmfidence Breath

When you are on shaky ground, anxious, and agitated, your breath can be short and shallow. The first thing you can do to regain your calm is to control your breathing. You've probably had someone tell you to "take a deep breath" when you are stressed. While this is good advice, keep in mind that it is not the inhale that brings you calm and control but the EXHALE that provides the release and relief.

MINDFUL BREATHING

Close your eyes and breathe in for four seconds, hold it for a beat ,and then breathe out slowly for a count of eight seconds. Put your attention on your breath and repeat to yourself: *Breathe in calm and confidence, breathe out stress and anxiety; breathe in calm and confidence, breathe out stress and anxiety.* Mindfully breathing in and out with a mantra like this will help you to get your breathing under control and also occupy your mind so there is no room for negative thoughts. As you breathe out, you can even visualize your exhale releasing worry, fear, negative thoughts and images, and anything else you want to evacuate from your body and mind.

BE A BELLY BREATHER

During one of my recent speaker training visits with the people at Gaia, a digital wellness TV network, renowned yogi Ashleigh Sergeant shared her number-one tip for controlling the fight-or-flight adrenaline response that many people feel under pressure: "Most people breathe from their chest when they are stressed, and the adrenaline ensures they stay there. Consciously taking slow deep breaths, expanding the belly, helps take back that control, calming both the body and mind," says Sergeant.

Belly breathing can be done while standing, sitting, or lying down. Breathe in slowly and deeply, concentrating the breath into your belly; then empty your belly slowly and completely. I've found that one very effective way to see and feel that you are belly breathing is to lie down on a comfortable surface and place an object on your navel—something that won't slide or roll off, such as a book or a stuffed animal. As you slowly and deeply breathe in and out, the item will rise and fall. Just the act of doing this exercise for a few minutes will bring you some Calmfidence.

Inspired Calmfidence Tools

There's a reason that cheerleaders, coaches, fans, mentors, and great motivational speakers exist in this world. Even the best athletes, leaders, and artists need inspiration. They need to get in the zone, get pumped, get their creative juices flowing, and have someone push them further than they think they can go. When they find themselves on shaky ground, they look to their coaches for support and guidance. The same is true for all of us. We all know that when someone believes in us we try harder, when we believe in ourselves we accomplish more, and when we have a friend rooting for us we can go further than we might have and overcome obstacles.

You can create your own personal cheering section, your very own team of coaches all around you, every day, to inspire Calmfidence in yourself and your goals. You can also condition yourself to be the best coach there is—your own! Here's how:

- Collect inspiring quotes. Print them out and hang them on your fridge, bulletin board, or dashboard. Put them on your screen saver and cell phone.

- Instead of listening to music or news in your car or on your iPod, load in audio books that pump you up, get you into a positive mindset, or teach you techniques about reaching goals or learning new skills. Having positive motivational messages pumped into your brain before a meeting, speech, interview, or new challenge can make a huge difference in the outcome.

- Your subconscious is like a sponge, and it loves to store anything that you feed it over and over again. We're really good at doing this with negative thoughts, but the opposite works just as well. Collect affirmations that you can repeat to yourself to push negativity out of your mind. I schedule daily affirmations on my calendar that pop up first thing in the morning and again in the afternoon on my cell phone to inspire me and remind me.

- Always carry a positive-thinking book with you, whether a print copy or one you downloaded onto your cell phone or device. When you are stuck somewhere waiting, if you have to eat alone somewhere or travel alone, read or listen to those uplifting, inspiring books.

- Keep a file for complimentary notes and letters. Fill it with any notes, letters, emails, positive reviews, thank-you cards, greeting cards, and love letters you've received. Go to this file when you need a little lift—you'll surprise yourself with the people you have touched.

- Subscribe to positive magazines and newsletters that are filled with inspiring stories, tips, and resources to help you reach your goals.

Calmfidence Ritual Tools

In chapter 1, "Calmfidence Boosters," we talked about examining your state of Calmfidence and how to boost yourself back up to a place where you feel calm and confidence. A Calmfidence ritual is a tool that performers use to get them into the zone, where they are at their best and ready to shine. These are especially useful when your heart rate goes up and those butterflies start zooming around in your belly.

The PBS American Masters documentary *Johnny Carson: King of Late Night* reveals that the late-night talk show host (who helmed NBC's *Tonight Show* for thirty years) had a nightly ritual before each show whereby he would pace behind the curtain as if he were waiting for a baby to be delivered. He needed to do this before emerging through the gap in the curtain and beginning his monologue; otherwise he did not feel ready to step into the spotlight. A popular news anchor I coach goes into the restroom before each of her live shows, gets down on one knee, and says a quick prayer to get into what she calls her solid place. A professional speaker I coached on many occasions meditates for thirty seconds while patting her belly the whole time. She says this gets her body and mind connected and present in the current moment. Here are some other rituals many of my clients use:

- Stand up tall. A strong upright posture will make you feel more powerful, and you will appear more powerful to others. Posture is one of the first outward signs to other people of how we feel about ourselves.

- Dig in your heels. Firmly plant your feet on the ground with your weight evenly distributed on each foot. Balance yourself and think of your feet as roots holding up an enormous, sturdy oak tree that can handle all the wind, rain, and thunder around it. This will help you feel more grounded.

- Trust yourself. I cannot say this enough. Repeat "I trust myself" to yourself.

- Remind yourself that there have been other times when you felt unsure, yet somehow you figured things out and got through.

- Visualize the last time you were in a state of Calmfidence. Close your eyes and feel the feelings you felt when you were at your best. Replay this record over and over in your mind's eye.

- Focus on the why. Why do you need or want to have Calmfidence in this situation? What is the outcome you desire, and why is it important to you? Is the outcome more important than a little discomfort? If it is, then focus on the outcome and do what you have to do to pull some Calmfidence from deep inside. If it's been there before, it's still there if you demand it from yourself.

- Don't allow others to rush you or get you flustered. You need to be able to think straight and only make decisions and choices when you feel ready and prepared to do so. If someone is trying to pressure you into doing something, call a time-out by stating that you need more time. Tell them that you do not rush into decisions.

- When on shaky ground—stand your ground!

Because we are talking about rituals that can help us when we feel anxious and stressed, I want to briefly talk about obsessive-compulsive disorder (OCD) here. Obsessive-compulsive disorder is a common *disorder* that can actually result in a lot of *order*, I have found. I have mild OCD, and quite a few of my clients have it too. People who experience anxiety can also have some level of OCD. It's hard for others who don't have OCD to understand our thought process, but I bet you know a friend or loved one who has it. OCD can actually be an asset because you can use rituals and repetitive affirmations to your advantage. When I want to remember things I'm studying, bullet points for a speech, or names or stats, I use my OCD "skills" to help me out. OCD made Denzel Washington a pretty awesome badass in the movie *The Equalizer* as he planned and organized his strategies for justice. I choose to look at my OCD as an asset and not a negative; doing so means that it works for me and not against me. I use it as one of my Calmfidence tools now. This is another great example of how you perceive yourself and your uniqueness as an individual can affect your calm and confidence for better or worse.

Rules of Calmfidence

Do you have rules for allowing yourself to have Calmfidence? I bet you do—and I bet you don't even know it. Often, we set ourselves up for failure and doubt because we have created negative rules in our own mind that don't exist but are very real to us. These negative rules really kick in when we are unsure of ourselves. Here are some common negative rules:

* I can have Calmfidence only when I look a certain way.
* I can have Calmfidence only once I am loved.
* I can have Calmfidence only when I am around people I know.
* I can have Calmfidence when I have a drink.
* I can have Calmfidence once I smoke a cigarette.
* I can have Calmfidence once I have more money.
* I can have Calmfidence once I get my degree.
* I can have Calmfidence once I get that promotion or job.

Are your personal Calmfidence rules holding you back? Think about what your rules are. Now ask yourself if they are helping you or hurting you. What criteria do you think you have to meet in order to have Calmfidence? Write down your answers, then ask yourself:

- Do these rules sound logical?
- Have other people given you your rules?
- Did your family or friends hand down these rules to you?
- Are you living by someone else's rules for Calmfidence?

Realize that your prerequisites for Calmfidence may just be ways for you to procrastinate or make excuses so that you don't have to take chances and put yourself out there to the world.

Going outside of your comfort zone is, well, uncomfortable—but it is the only way to grow and become more than you are right now. If you are not feeling discomfort, you are probably not growing and expanding. Know that you will feel uncomfortable, and work through it. Get comfortable with feeling uncomfortable.

Give yourself permission to create some new positive rules that will empower you. Test them out slowly. Do small things each day to break some old rules, adding your new rules a little at a time at first. Here are a few examples:

- I can have Calmfidence because I am unique.
- I can have Calmfidence because I am caring.
- I can have Calmfidence because my intentions are good.
- I can have Calmfidence because I have come this far already.
- I can have Calmfidence because I work hard to do my best.
- I can have Calmfidence because I have just as much right to have it as anyone else.

Notice what happens after you change some of your old negative rules. Does the world stop? Does chaos ensue? Do you die from embarrassment? Probably not. But your world might change, for the better.

Calmfidence Control When on Shaky Ground

Self-control is a major factor when it comes to Calmfidence. You can have high self-esteem and believe in yourself, but if you can't control your emotions, actions, and responses, being successful is going to be harder for you, if not impossible, when you are out of your comfort zone.

Discipline, persistence, personal high standards, integrity, respect for yourself, and respect for others all determine if your Calmfidence is built on a solid foundation. Recognize that instant gratification rarely has positive results. A quick fix for anything usually doesn't last.

Part of controlling our emotions and thoughts is learning to *respond* to people and situations instead of *reacting* to them. These sound similar yet are very different. When you react, you usually do it quickly; you may have a knee-jerk reaction, a subconscious, primitive impulse. When you respond, however, you are choosing how you will handle your reaction; you're making a clear, well-thought-out choice on how to proceed. In making a response, you think before you blurt out something. In making a response, you keep yourself from making assumptions and jumping to conclusions. Making a response helps you to ask questions calmly and to collect more information so that you can make a more informed choice on how to handle a person or a situation better.

Decide what you want to have happen ahead of time. My father always taught me to make up my mind about what I was going to do in any situation *before* I got into the situation. He believed this would help me to not be swayed by others' opinions, not be influenced by other people's desires, or make any decisions that I didn't think through and might regret later. This worked well for me growing up, especially when I found myself in challenging situations.

Here are some other factors that help to increase Calmfidence when you find yourself on shaky ground:

- Keep your word. Commit to things even if you no longer have the motivation to do them.
- Do what you say you are going to do.
- Control your mental dialogue.

- Be patient.

- Don't fall for instant gratification.

- Understand that most things are a process.

- Pace yourself.

- Don't prejudge.

- Have a plan and follow it . . .

- (But) stay flexible.

- Control your outlook—being an optimist or a pessimist is a CHOICE.

- Stay calm and regroup if you go off track.

- Be willing to give up control when it comes to things you really can't control anyway.

- Know that you are the only one who is in complete control of your Calmfidence level.

- Turn up the heat slowly. People tend to tolerate things that happen slowly rather than just jumping into a heated situation and getting burned. The same goes for public speaking, speaking up for yourself, or mustering up the courage to ask for a raise or a date. The more you do it, the more you put yourself out there, the more chances you take, the more you will get desensitized to the unsettling feelings and growing pains.

Calmfidence Tools to Help You Prepare

PRE-PAVED CALMFIDENCE

When you know you are headed for shaky ground—whether it's a conversation you've been dreading with your boss, a speech you've been asked to give, or a situation you've been trying to avoid—visualize what you *want* to happen. Only choose positive images to visualize. Many people are really good at visualizing, but unfortunately, they tend to visualize things going wrong. It's a human default to quickly imagine and create images of what could go wrong. This is a defense mechanism, a primitive way of quickly preparing ourselves with a plan if something bad happens. It's a survival instinct.

The problem with this instinctive reaction is that most of the bad things we visualize never actually happen, but we live them in our minds like they have. This causes stress and anxiety. We prepare for the worst and get ourselves in that state of fight-or-flight. This is fine if you're walking down a dark street alone at night, but when it comes to public speaking, communicating with friends and family, or dealing with coworkers, it's much more beneficial to envision things going well.

Create a visual plan in your mind of what you want to happen. This way you will go into a situation positive and strong. Even if something goes wrong you can deal with it from a sturdier, calmer place rather than a place of agitation. This positive visual plan is known as *pre-paving*—like paving a road before you travel on it.

When I train clients on pre-paving and visualization, I always use the analogy of an airline pilot. Commercial airline pilots not only have a copilot but also pre-program the plane's autopilot to follow the flight plan to get everyone on board safely to their destination. Programmed correctly, that plane can even land itself. So, if a pilot has a heart attack during the flight, the copilot can take over and/or the flight plan will still operate.

You have to think of your subconscious as your copilot or autopilot. Your subconscious is that primitive place deep in your mind that has listened carefully to each plan you have given it, intentionally or not. The last thing you say to yourself right before a stressful event is going to be the last plan your subconscious has been preprogrammed with. Garbage in equals garbage out. Don't let your brain default to a bad plan that has images of things going wrong. Make sure it has a fully visualized plan of positive self-talk and images so that you continue to fly without a hitch.

GUIDED IMAGERY

When on shaky ground, work out your mind muscle! I studied guided imagery in a certificate program with psychologist Dr. Thomas Nardi in order to help my clients and students visualize success in public speaking, and to better deal with performance anxiety. Basically, guided imagery taps into the idea that the body goes where the mind goes. Many of the athletes I work with tell me they never go into a game or take a shot without first seeing themselves winning in their mind's eye *ahead* of time. Next time you are about to go into a stressful situation, try bombarding your mind with images of what you want to have happen instead of what you don't want to have happen.

HOMEWORK AND LEGWORK

When you are about to embark on something stressful or challenging, nothing gives you more Calmfidence than knowing you've done your research. You will feel much more sturdy knowing you've tried to find out everything about a situation before you get into it. Most people are very unsettled when they don't know what they are up against or when they feel that other people know more about something than they do. Do your homework on people, places, events, companies, products, services, and so on before you get into a situation instead of waiting to see what's going on once you get there. It's so easy these days to pop just about anything or anyone into a search engine and get some insight into who they are, or what something is all about. Think of yourself as an investigative reporter. Information, knowledge, and know-how are a huge component to feeling Calmfidence when in shaky territory.

EAT THE ELEPHANT

In acting, performers use a technique when trying to memorize a large script called Eating the Elephant. The actor who is told they have to memorize a two-hundred-page script would never be able to do so if they tried to do it all at once. No one can eat an elephant whole, but if you start with the toe, move on to the foot, then the leg, and so on, eventually you could consume it all. So they eat the elephant. They get one small section down; then and only then do they add the next small section. They do it in steps. Likewise, when something seems so large and daunting that it puts you on shaky ground, break it down into chunks to make it more manageable. The most important thing about doing things in digestible bites is that you get moving in the right direction, and action keeps you from getting stuck. Getting overwhelmed makes most people freeze, but so does inaction.

PRACTICE

Most people aren't good at things until they practice. Most things in life are a process. Situations improve over time. First we find our rhythm, then we uncover little nuances. Usually there is no short cut to getting good at something. You've got to put in your time. Repetition, fine-tuning, and uncovering what works for you and what doesn't takes time. Great athletes and performers can only make true magic once they get the basics down so deep that they no longer have to think of them. It's what Malcolm Gladwell refers to in his book *Outliers*: the most amazing achievers at the top of their games have generally put ten thousand hours into whatever it is that they are great at.

Now, don't get overwhelmed and think "I don't have ten thousand hours" or "I can't wait until those ten thousand hours take place." The point here is to keep practicing whatever it is that you want to get good at. You *will* get better.

FILM YOUR PRACTICE

You can be your own best coach. When you are trying to learn something visual or auditory, a video camera or your phone's video function is your best friend. Don't hide from it; embrace it. I've been fascinated by recording video since I was a kid. The idea that we can capture our lives like a movie, so we can keep moments alive long after they are over, is pure magic to me. I love that when we watch and hear ourselves, we get an outside view and see what others see. This is a scary thing to many people because they aren't used to seeing themselves from this perspective. Once we get used to watching ourselves and knowing what we sound like, we can use this tool to our advantage. Whether it's a recording of your golf swing, your interview skills, or you speaking in public, you have now captured your form, body language, voice, facial expression, energy, and vibe, and you can pause, rewind, and fast-forward to deconstruct your skills and make the weak ones stronger—and the strong ones stronger too.

Now that we've explored ways to build our resilience utilizing Calmfidence tools and I've got you in front of the camera, let's take a closer look at "Self-Image Calmfidence" in chapter 7.

A Client's Story

Joy was an acting teacher in the heart of the theater district in New York City. We taught classes at the same well-known performing arts school near Times Square. Joy really was a joy. She wasn't teaching because she needed the money. She really wanted to see her students shine and thrive in a tough business. Her weekend workshops were constantly sold out, largely through word of mouth, because her students genuinely loved her and she loved them.

Yet on one weekend, she didn't get the usual turnout, and she got wind that another teacher's weekend workshops were becoming popular. Some of Joy's regular students had attended that one instead. This other teacher was a casting director who flew in from the West Coast a few times a year. She had been talking down Joy in her class, even as she was condescending to the students, checked her cell phone constantly, and took frequent cigarette breaks. The students put up with her unprofessionalism because a casting director could help them get auditions, and auditions lead to work that pays the bills.

After the West Coast teacher's workshop, each and every one of Joy's students reached out to Joy to let her know how the casting director was trying to undermine her good work and growing reputation. Joy was shocked. She not only knew this casting director but had taken one of her classes when she was just starting out in the industry. Joy reached out by phone in hopes of talking with her, but she never received a return call. Joy started to wonder if maybe what the casting director said was true—that her own acting experience was too limited for her to be able to help others.

When Joy talked to me about what was going on, I almost fell over. How could she doubt herself when hundreds of students were singing her praises and constantly sending her thank-you cards and emails? So often we don't see our own value. If we are humble, we minimize our accomplishments or don't even recognize them because we just aren't used to tooting our own horn. So I asked Joy to sit down and do a brain dump on paper of all of the acting roles she had over the past fifteen years. "What's the point?" Joy said in a discouraged tone. "You'll see," I said. After about ten minutes she had several pages filled. "You're gonna run out of ink!" I said and laughed at Joy as her list of accomplishments grew and grew. After she had transitioned to teaching, she hadn't looked at or updated her acting résumé. Once Joy got everything on paper that she could think of, she looked through the filled notebook and said, "Wow, I can't believe this is ME!" There had been so many acting roles over the years that she had forgotten about. Joy's experience was enormous. That snarky casting director had actually done Joy a huge favor. Joy might not have ever taken the time to take a personal inventory of her experiences, skills, and talents if that smack-down hadn't happened.

Joy used this new perspective and information in all of her marketing materials, on her website, and in her newsletters. Workshops and class demand grew even more after that, and Joy was able to reach and help even more students.

Calmfidence Reflections

List three things you could put on your Calmfidence credit card:

_____

_____

_____

Create three positive rules of Calmfidence you can follow:

_____

_____

_____

List three Calmfidence rituals you can create:

_____

_____

_____

7

Self-Image
Calmfidence

There is a Fountain of Youth: it is your mind, your talents, the
creativity you bring to your life and the lives of people you love.
When you learn to tap this source, you will truly have defeated age.

Sophia Loren

Resilience is our ability to recover from difficulties quickly. Grit is the
strength of our character where our courage comes from. I wanted
this part of our journey on resilient Calmfidence to be about self-image
because it is often the part of us that takes a beating when we go through
major changes or challenges in our lives. How our mind, talents, and
creativity serve us and those we love gives us purpose and passion from
the same internal spring that Calmfidence flows from. But it's easy to
get hung up on our self-image and outward appearance. Our opinion
of ourselves can be vastly different from how others actually perceive us.
Until we grow in Calmfidence, our self-perception can be negative and
minimizing—and often the opposite of how others actually see us.

When Cassandra walked into my training room, I thought she looked
the image of someone who was successful and in charge. She was classy,
well dressed, and looked like a person of influence. But I soon learned
she had a completely different inner image of herself. She was filled with
self-doubt about both her personal and professional life. "After being out
of the work force for several years to raise my children, I've lost much of

my confidence. I don't feel good about the way that I look. My body has changed. I've been communicating in mommy speech and not business speech," she admitted. "I'm overwhelmed by the thought of speaking in public and being in the spotlight in any way. I don't feel like I'm at the same level as the people I'm now working with."

As part of her new job, Cassandra had been asked to chair a hospital foundation fundraiser and emcee its prominent dinner event, which would put her in front of hundreds of hospital executives and physicians. She would also be the face of the promotions leading up to the event, which included a big photo shoot. Talk about being thrown right into the fire as she reentered the professional world. She was terrified that she didn't match the role she was being asked to fill and was minimizing herself and her abilities. Throughout our sessions Cassandra was able to take an inventory of her experiences and strengths, to refocus her valuation of her talents, and to build up confidence once again. She began to take chances and think more positive thoughts: "I had a powerful realization. I began to see that I had a lesser opinion of myself than others did of me. This was an incredible turning point for me, my self-esteem, confidence, and reaching my goals. I started to tap into my personal strength and inner trust and see myself in a new light." I attended the hospital foundation dinner the night Cassandra served as emcee. She was glowing. Her voice and body language exuded confidence at the podium. She knew her value. You could see she just felt good about herself. Everyone in the room responded in kind.

In the following pages we'll look at four areas where our Calmfidence gets put to the test when it comes to our self-image.

Age Calmfidence

Age is a tricky and often touchy subject. We use it as a convenient self-sabotaging weapon at just about every stage of our lives. Do either of these sound familiar? "I'm too young—I'll never be taken seriously"; "I'm too old—they'll want someone younger." At any stage in our lives we can easily use the excuse of age to stop us from trying something new, from fulfilling a dream, or simply being happy in the now. The only way to stop this self-sabotage is to make a conscious choice to declare that you are the right age for right now. This is the only reality there is, isn't it? You can't be younger or older than you are right now. You simply can't change the number, but you can change the thoughts you think and the way you live your life.

I was hired by a fashion designer to help her communicate better and feel calmer and more confident during television appearances. She was about ten to fifteen years older than me and was concerned about her age influencing how she would look and feel in front of the camera. I look younger than I am, and my client was surprised when I told her how old I was. She told me that when she first considered hiring me she thought I might be too young to have the experience and wisdom she was looking for in a coach and trainer. We had a good laugh over it, and she insisted that I post my age on my website and materials so that my younger appearance didn't deter prospective clients from hiring me. The funniest part was that I had recently turned fifty and was wrapping my mind around this new *older* decade.

The moral of this story is that we all perceive things very differently. To some people being too young is a problem. To others being too old is a problem. It's all relative to each individual situation.

Another client of mine, a CEO of a large marketing company, was struggling with giving presentations to his employees because at age thirty-five he felt his employees would judge him as not ready to lead them the way a more seasoned (older) CEO might. He would come into our one-on-one public-speaking sessions and joke that he just needed me to give him a "therapy session" to get over it. Over time we were able to work through the fact that he simply could not do anything about changing his age. Through our work he eventually got past his concern and decided to spend his energy focusing on the fact that his company was doing very well and his employees were all generally happy working for him.

Yet another client, a wonderful CEO of a large chain store who I helped prepare for his company's one-hundredth anniversary celebration, was concerned that he was looking and sounding older now that he was in his seventies. None of his thousands of employees could have cared less about his age. He was the only one worrying about it. He was so beloved by everyone that just by walking onto the stage he received a rock-star's welcome. We worked on helping him get out of his own way by taking his mental spotlight off of himself and shining it bright on his great employees.

Here are some things you can do right now to have more Calmfidence at any age or stage of life:

- If you're young and inexperienced, think of yourself as a fresh face, an eager learner, a clean slate, or a sponge ready to give your all to your work, your dreams, and the people in your life. Don't focus on your lack of experience, but rather on your fresh perspective and energy.

- If you've been around the block and have lived a little (or a lot), focus on the wisdom you have gained, the experiences that have molded you, and the unique knowledge that you have acquired that only comes with time.

- Don't focus on wanting to stay or look young; instead focus on staying and looking *current and polished*. Don't get stuck in any one stage, style, or era. Keep moving forward. Reinvent, redefine, and refine! Focus on looking and feeling healthy, vibrant, and well rested to the best of your ability through your choices, habits, and outlook.

- If you tell yourself you're too young, then you are. If you tell yourself you're too old, then you are. Either complaint is just an excuse.

- Know that there are pros and cons at every single age—and that you and only you are in charge of what you choose to focus on or where your attention leads you. Whether you focus on your pros or your cons, your focus becomes your reality.

- Take charge. Take action. Take the age number out of the equation and create the life you want in each moment. Demand to learn and grow at every age.

- Concentrate on health, not numbers. A positive attitude about age (at any age) can contribute to a longer, happier life—even more than low cholesterol or regular exercise.

- As comedian George Carlin once said, "Age is only mind over matter. If you don't mind . . . it doesn't matter."

Body Calmfidence

Like it or not, your body does have an impact on how you feel about yourself. Having Calmfidence living in your own body is important. After all, it's the only one you've got. You can't have someone else's. It's your billboard to the world. Once you make friends with your body and really learn to love it, you end up taking better care of it—and, in turn, it takes better care of you.

Look around at all the famous people you know who are not physically perfect. There are short people, fat people, strange-looking people, and downright unattractive people. Do you think they were focusing on their bodies and faces on their journey to become famous? Maybe, but they forged ahead anyway. They were focusing on being a great actor, a great comic, a great artist, a great singer, and so on. We don't care what they look like. We are so attracted to their talent that it overshadows everything else.

We can do this in our own lives, by thinking positive productive thoughts. Creative thoughts, expressive thoughts, artistic thoughts, successful thoughts, determined thoughts, thoughts on how to get better at what we do. I'm sure those celebrities all had their moments when they wished that their faces or bodies looked different, maybe fit some kind of mold of what society calls beauty, but what won out was they had more beauty inside of them than on the outside and they stayed persistent with their dreams and goals.

If you had to choose, which would you pick: a life where your face and body are perfect but there's not much going on inside? No creativity, no passion, no romance, no drive, no screaming that pushes you forward to be amazing at the thing you choose to express during your time in this life? Or would you choose less physical perfection and a wonderful rich outlook on life?

You have probably met people throughout your life who you didn't find attractive at first, but once you got to know them you were attracted to them.

It's all about energy. Positive life-force energy overpowers anything that our external self has to offer. When we concentrate on striving to make that inner life-force energy all that it can be, our outside really doesn't matter much anymore. As a matter of fact, the outside will glow from the inner energy. The opposite of this is also true. Pretty people can become ugly to us really fast if they have a rotten or empty inside.

We are so much more than what others see at first glance. Focus on creating, growing, and exploding your energy into this world, and don't put so much emphasis on the vehicle we call a body that happens to be taking you on this journey. Sure, take care of it, respect it, but if it's different than what society calls perfect or attractive, let it go. Accept it. Embrace it and shine from the inside out!

Here are some things you can do right now to have more body Calmfidence:

- When you're alone, take a minute to really look at yourself in the mirror. Look at yourself to see yourself in all your glory. The human body really is a beautiful work of art.

- Look at the strength of your body, the beauty of your skin; be thankful for the eyes that allow you to see all the wonderful things in the world and the power of your ears that help you hear the voices of those you love and the friends you have.

- Thank your body for getting you this far this well.

Unrealistic Calmfidence

Your self-image concerns are actually competing with outside images that are not real. Keep in mind that so many of the images we see in the media and on the web are manipulated, retouched, and enhanced by apps and digital tools and hair-and-makeup teams, so that we really don't know what reality is anymore.

The first time I had professional headshots taken in New York City, the photographer allowed me to look through his portfolio book, which included photos of many celebrities before they'd been retouched. I was shocked to see the original photos with the lines, wrinkles, and flawed skin that made them look more like average people. It made me feel good and bad simultaneously! Even for women in their early twenties it was recommended that every headshot be retouched—the acne, dark circles, scars, and smile lines all removed or softened.

I ran into a guy I'd gone to high school with who is working in advertising. He told me that they digitally stretch and lengthen limbs and necks on models' pictures, and they erase the sides of jeans in the outer and inner thigh areas to make celebrities and models appear thinner. He said it was like playing with the Stretch Armstrong and Gumby toys he had as a kid.

Photographers tell me that for one photo shoot of a celebrity or model they take hundreds of shots just to get one good cover shot or headshot for a project. And at every photo shoot, makeup artists, hair stylists, and wardrobe people get the model or celebrity ready prior to the shoot. The lighting, background, and people who aim blowing air from fans are also hard at work making everything look perfect.

Many models, performers, and celebrities diet the whole time they are shooting a project, only to binge the minute the production wraps. So basically, what we see is the final product of best behavior with a slew of people helping them look larger than life. Yet regular Joes and Jills try to live up to these images, which are not even reality. This is especially important for young people to understand. There are a few websites that will allow you to see what was retouched in a photo by moving your mouse back and forth across the image.

Even on social media the majority of people only post the pictures and videos they want you to see. Rarely do you see images of someone's "bad hair" day, weak moments, or perceived flaws. Everyone's lives look pretty good on social media. In entertainment and television, these are called highlight reels or sizzle reels. These are the very best video clips and images of a person edited together to show an overview of that person's experiences and performances. Only the strongest, most flattering images and clips make the cut. The end result should "sizzle" and make the viewer want to work with them or hire them. The flubs, less-than-perfect moments, bad lighting, and anything undesirable get edited out.

Here are some things you can do right now to have more realistic Calmfidence:

- Embrace your flaws.
- Don't compare yourself to images that are designed to sell you something by making you feel like you aren't enough.
- Remind yourself that most of the images you see every day have been manipulated and enhanced to look perfect.

Posing for Calmfidence

Many of my clients need to have professional pictures taken for their work. Many executives and experts have no desire to smile for the camera, but they have to pose for this "necessary evil." Some have told me that they shun the camera and hate to have their picture taken even at family gatherings. The reason they usually end up disliking their photos is because of how they were feeling while their picture was being taken. The discomfort, awkwardness, and dislike come shining through.

Here are some tips to help you become friends with the camera:

- Practice your facial expressions ahead of time in the mirror. Then, during the photo session, remember which expressions you find most pleasing and work with the photographer to incorporate them into the shoot.

- The camera knows what you are thinking. My father always told me this when I was starting out in my career. If you hate every moment of the process, the camera will document this in detail. If you are expecting bad results, you will get them. Your facial expression must be genuine and natural. Therefore, as the photographer is snapping away, do whatever it takes to visualize people you love, clients you want, and the impressions you want to give. Your face must say something real. Think of memories or things to come that bring a true smile to your face, in the moment, so that the photographer can capture them. Think about puppies, chocolate, or dollar signs!

- It will really help you if you practice finding your comfort zone in casual family photography situations. Don't run and hide when a family member starts taking pictures at a family gathering. This is the worst thing you can do. You are not giving yourself what you need to relax and be playful with the camera, with your family, with life. Photos are truly a blessing and something to cherish as time goes by.

- Pick your makeup artist and hair stylist carefully. I suggest you visit stylists ahead of time and have full hair and makeup done prior to the shoot to ensure you like how you will look and that you are comfortable and feel like yourself—you don't want to feel like you are wearing a mask or being someone you are not. Once you are satisfied with the results, schedule these people for the actual shoot. (PS: Men need their hair styled and some makeup for the camera too.)

- Pick your photographer carefully. Just because they say they are good, or someone else says they are good, does not mean they are a good fit for you. Look through their portfolios to see if they have photographed people who have the same coloring and style as you. Notice the lighting and the use of shadows and contrast. And pay attention to the background; is it static and blank, or interesting, contemporary, and fresh?

- Bring some favorite snapshots to your first meeting with the photographer. He or she doesn't know you; they don't know how you normally look, and most importantly they don't know how you "see" yourself. Only bring photos of yourself that you like. Explain why you like them. Let the photographer get to know you through your pictures. Even if you are saying right now that you dislike every picture of you ever taken, there must be at least one snapshot somewhere that you like of yourself.

- Your clothing is important. Try to pick items that work year-round and in all time zones. Solid jewel tones work best on all skin tones. Wear colors that people usually compliment you on when you wear them. Pay attention to necklines that work for you in everyday life and that you feel comfortable in.

- Avoid busy patterns, very dark or very light tones, and big or shiny jewelry (consider eliminating jewelry altogether, as it can quickly grow "dated" and tends to be distracting). You want people to see your eyes and face first, not your jewelry or clothes.

- When we look in the mirror, we are seeing the reverse image of ourselves, so that's what seems normal to us. When we see a photograph, it is the opposite of what we are used to seeing in the mirror—and we need to adjust our mind to this fact.

The more photos you take and allow others to take of you, the more comfortable you will get seeing yourself in pictures. If you regularly avoid having your photograph taken, you are doing yourself a disservice and you will never achieve this comfort level.

- This is not about vanity. Pictures are necessary business tools: people want to be able to put a face to a name, to a résumé, to a company, to a brand. Your photograph is a marketing tool, a human connector that should make people want to meet you, get to know you, trust you, invest in you. Allow yourself the opportunity to make your photo a good one that you are proud of, comfortable with, and happy with, by doing your research, preparing, and cultivating the proper mindset you need to get a great shot.

- Finally, like most things, your picture will grow on you. When you first see your shots, they may seem foreign, sometimes like an out-of-body experience. We are so much more than a frozen snapshot in time. Our energy, movement, mannerisms, and personality can't possibly be summed up in one photograph. By using the above tips you'll have the best shot at capturing a more accurate glimpse of you, one you'll want to share with the world.

Now that we've covered ways you can grow your resilience with self-image Calmfidence, let's explore another area where grit and resilience is key—pursuing your goals!

Calmfidence Reflections

List three things you like about your current age:

_____

_____

_____

List three things you like about your body:

_____

_____

_____

List three things you like about your face:

_____

_____

_____

List three things you like about your style:

_____

_____

_____

List two perceived "imperfections" that you can embrace and celebrate:

_____

_____

8

Calmfidence Goals

Life isn't about finding yourself.
Life is about creating yourself.
George Bernard Shaw

If there's a time we all need resilience and Calmfidence, it's when we are trying to reach our goals. Many years ago I approached a local radio station with an idea for a talk show about ways people could communicate with confidence. It was called "Inside and Out" with Patricia Stark. It was the dream show I had always hoped would come along but hadn't, so I needed to create it myself. It was on a very small AM radio station along the Hudson River Valley, upstate from New York City, and I was a one-woman band: producer, writer, sponsor locator, promoter, and host. I covered all kinds of topics on confidence, self-talk, positive thinking, communication skills, body language, stress and anxiety relievers, all of the things I write about in this book. I booked and interviewed guest experts, talked about all the coaching and training strategies I used with my clients and students, and opened up the lines to take questions even though I really didn't get many. I loved every minute of it, but it felt like I was making little impact. Each time the on-air light turned red and the big silver microphone stared me in the face, I thought, *Is anybody even listening?* Ernie Anastos, an iconic and beloved news anchor and a fixture in New York City for decades, somehow stumbled upon the work I was doing on my little radio show. "Hello, Patricia!" he exclaimed in his deep booming voice when I answered my cell phone. "I've been listening to your radio show and I love everything you are doing! I'd like to have you on my 6 p.m. newscast as a guest expert to talk about some of the topics you've been covering."

Here I'd thought no one was listening. This was the beginning of what would turn into a tremendous friendship. I appeared on Ernie's newscast dozens of times as I was developing and growing what would become my Calmfidence brand of coaching and training.

The bottom line: create work you love, build it, and they will come. Take action. Even when your baby steps seem small, even when it feels like no one is listening, or even cares, know that you are planting seeds and keep tending to your garden.

Let's turn now to some of the best ways to reach your goals and build your resilience.

Get Out There

One of my favorite quotes is from Josiah Gilbert Holland, who wrote, "God gives every bird its food, but He does not throw it into its nest." Think of how true this is. It's all out there. Food for birds is everywhere, but they have to go get it. No one is delivering it to them. But leaving the safety of their nest is dangerous. They might get eaten by another animal or die in a storm or fly into a window. But if birds don't leave their nests to find food, they will surely starve to death. The birds that are really bold make friends with humans who are happy to throw food to them. It reminds me of people who want to help other people when they see them spreading their wings, showing initiative, a go-getter attitude, determination, and personal responsibility. I love feeding the birds and squirrels in my backyard every morning because they come all around me; they aren't afraid. One squirrel even taps on my back door each morning and takes a slice of bread from my hand like from a fast-food drive-thru window! This squirrel impresses me, so of course I want to give it an extra treat. This is how the world responds to people who take action and create opportunities for themselves.

Keep Going

Never give up. I once saw an actor who appeared as a guest on a late-night talk show who was introduced as an overnight success. The actor laughed when he sat down and said, "Yeah, an overnight success. I've been doing this for fifteen years and nobody ever heard of me until now."

People give up too soon. They don't stay focused long enough; they let themselves get discouraged. When they do that, they actually create room for the other people who don't give up. If you want something and are willing to work hard for it, it has to eventually come if you stay the course and don't take no for an answer. There can be a lot of perks that come with reaching your goals later than planned. Maturity, comfort level, and an inner calm seem to be something late bloomers have in common. Most late bloomers I've worked with don't sweat the small stuff or get rattled very easily.

Create Your Calmfidence Standards

You are the boss of your life. If you were going to hire someone to do a job for you, would you want them to just give you their minimum effort and do an average job, or would you want to have someone who takes pride in what they do, someone who has a passion, who has positive energy? People who take ownership of their work always seem to move up and on to bigger and better things. Don't do your job just to satisfy others. Don't live your life for others. Don't discount yourself; don't sell yourself short. Live up to your own standards for yourself, because you are worth it. It's through effort and care that we earn friendship, health, wealth, and peace of mind. When you aim high and set high standards for yourself and you value yourself, you end up bringing great value to other people. People will want you around, and they'll want to help you reach the top. Don't just take up space. Don't wait for what life gives you. You have to ask for what you want and be willing to earn it. Stand out from the crowd by having high standards for yourself.

A lot of people just don't figure things out for themselves and get moving. They tend to want things spelled out for them or they want someone to hold their hand and walk them through it. They may even ask "why me" or complain that a task is not in their job description. You want to have the "plus factor," a combination of self-motivation and determination. Going the extra mile, doing more than is expected of you, and being more than the bare-minimum guy or gal can bring you enormous success. Having this plus factor actually builds your Calmfidence. It gives you the ability to take charge and get things done without having to have your hand held like a child. When you have the plus factor, you'll really stand out from the crowd and the competition.

Create Your Own Work

Once upon a time, getting a job with a good solid company meant job security. These days that's unfortunately not true anymore. We simply don't have a large amount of control over our own work destiny when we work for someone else. Yet most of us are taught by our schools and families that we should get a good education, find a good job with a good company, and we'll be all set. How wonderful it would be if our school years taught us how to create our own work, visualize and realize our own business—something we love to do. Today many freelancers whom I work with feel that their careers are more secure because they work with multiple people and companies and have various projects and many irons in the fire at the same time. If one goes away, there is another one right around the corner.

What could you create of your own? What skill, service, or idea will allow you to be the master of your own destiny in a career that you love, where work often feels like fun and not work? Do it in your spare time until you can do it full time.

Think About What You Would Do for Free

First, think about something you really have a passion for. Then think about something you love to do so much that you would actually do it for free. Then find a way to learn everything you can about it. Research others who are doing it or something similar. Buy every book on the topic that you can get your hands on. Search the internet for educational resources that offer online classes, certificates, or degrees related to your passion.

Master It!

Do everything you can in your spare time to get really good at something you're passionate about. Surround yourself with others who share your passion. Join groups or organizations that relate to it. Think of ways you could use it to help bring value to other people's lives. While you are honing your skills, do it for free. Do such an amazing job that people will tell others about what you do.

When you love what you do, and you get really good at it, people will want you—and they'll want to pay you—for your expertise.

What's your passion? Focus on it as if you're holding a magnifying glass in the sun to it and watch it ignite. Match it with a way to help people, and you'll have the Calmfidence to create your own work—which might not even feel like work.

Ask Why Not You?

So often we see other people doing the things we want to do and we get down on ourselves. We think, *How come them and not me?* Or we get discouraged thinking that we are not so lucky, haven't gotten a break, or we're not good enough, and that's why it's not happening for us. But when we do this, we are looking at things backward and inside out. Just the fact that other people are doing "it" should encourage us to know that it is possible, that it can be done. After all, someone is in fact doing it, so therefore it is attainable.

Plant Seeds

Many of my clients and students come to me for career guidance in addition to learning communication skills. Where do they go now? What next? How do they get the word out that they are ready for the world now that they have the training? Many of them want to get an agent or publicist. While both can help them get in front of the right people, I always stress that no one will work as hard for them as they will work for themselves. Ultimately, we cannot expect anyone else to consider us his or her top priority.

Your destiny is in your own hands, and you must make yourself your top priority. It's time to plant some seeds. Get the process going and growing! If every day you plant just one seed, you may find you have a crop on your hands in no time. Just before I left my full-time job as a producer/talent at a local TV station to work as a freelancer, I collected contact information for more than three hundred production companies within a fifty-mile radius of where I live. I mailed every one of them my materials. I knew I couldn't expect instant work, but I was planting seeds. A couple of them called me for freelance projects shortly after, but to my surprise some called months later and even a year later to say they kept my materials on file and finally had something they thought I might be right for. This was a great lesson for me. It made me realize that not hearing back from a job or a prospect doesn't mean no; it just might mean not right now.

Throw Sh#t Against the Wall
Until Some of It Sticks!

My father used to tell me, "If you throw enough sh#t against the wall, something's gotta stick!" This doesn't mean that you haphazardly reach for your goals in an unfocused way. It means that you must decide where you want to be and when you want to be there, then spray the infield, tackle it, don't take no for an answer, and put yourself and your goals out there for all to see! Direct marketers are thrilled when they get a 10 percent response rate on mailers or promotional materials. The more people you reach out to, the better your chances of stirring interest somewhere.

There is a great story about author Stephen King and his first novel, *Carrie*. The story goes that he had submitted his first manuscript of *Carrie* dozens of times to publishers, only to be told no time after time after time. He eventually got discouraged and actually threw the manuscript in the garbage. His wife believed in him and his work, and she fished it out of the garbage and submitted it to another publisher, who loved it. The rest is history. We never know how close we are to getting something to stick.

Anticipate Obstacles

There will be obstacles, no doubt. Count on them. If they make you give up, maybe you really didn't want it bad enough. If you momentarily let discouragement in, don't let it take residence. Give it a swift kick and boot it out the door. There will be people who will tell you every reason under the sun why you can't do something and why something won't work. They'll say there is too much competition. But the world has shown us many stories and examples of people who ignored the naysayers and succeeded. Be one of them.

Now that I have hopefully gotten you fired up about reaching your goals, it's the perfect time to move into part 3 of our journey, "Communication Calmfidence." To help you reach your goals and communicate with more Calmfidence in your daily life, I'll give you an abundance of ways you can build self-trust in your internal and external communication skills and interpersonal skills. These include strategies for more positive powerful self-talk, improving your speaking voice, confident eye-contact tips, and learning empowering nonverbal communication skills like facial expression and body language, right through to successfully handling that big speech or interview. Let's go!

Calmfidence Reflections

List three kinds of work that you would do even if no one could pay you:

_____

_____

_____

List three people who are doing something you would love to do:

_____

_____

_____

What are three ways you can research your goals and dreams?

_____

_____

_____

List three ways you could get good at your passion or something you love to do:

_____

_____

_____

Calmfidence

Part Three

Communication
Calmfidence

9

The Inner Voice
of Calmfidence

It's not what you say out of your mouth that determines your
life, it's what you whisper to yourself that has the most power.

Robert Kiyosaki

The most important thing you will ever hear is what you say to yourself. As
I said in the beginning of this book and it's important to repeat here,
Calmfidence doesn't come from what happens to you, it comes from what
happens in you. How do you speak to yourself? We all have two inner
voices: our inner critic and our inner coach. It takes no effort at all to
listen to our inner critic. It's easy to believe the negative voice and repeat
the negative stories. It takes a lot of practice and desire to talk to yourself
as a positive encouraging coach.

We filter outside voices through these two internal voices as well. No
matter what someone else says to us, we are always interpreting its meaning
based on our inner critic or inner coach, our perceptions, and our belief
system. We often give meaning to what other people say although we may
not interpret that meaning to be what they actually intended. We make
assumptions and come to conclusions based on our past experience, how
we feel about ourselves, how we feel about them, and how we feel about life.

When it comes to goals, success, and failure, we often say no to ourselves before we give other people a chance to make their own decisions
about us. We assume that people would not hire us, not like us, not

invest in us, or not believe in us before we even ask them. We make that decision in our mind and not in the real world. This prevents us from trying. It prevents us from pushing forward. It prevents us from being persistent. If we stop when we hear ourselves say no, how could we ever hope to break through barriers when others tell us no?

Seventy Percent of Self-Talk Is Negative

According to *Psychology Today*, 70 percent of self-talk is negative. On top of that, our subconscious is paying close attention. It absorbs whatever we are telling it. Repetition cements these thoughts deep inside. We think negative thoughts over and over again until they stick, even if they are not true.

There are many things that you cannot control in life, but you can control your own mind. Being a pessimist or an optimist may partially be the result of your upbringing, possibly built into your DNA, but at some point as you become a responsible adult, you have to take responsibility for how you use your brain. Eventually you choose to stay pessimistic or to become an optimist. It's nearly impossible to think a positive and a negative thought at the same time. You get to choose. Repetition is the cement that locks things into your subconscious. You have to work at overriding the negative thoughts by reciting positive statements over and over again. You also have to mean it. You have to feel it. What you choose to focus on eventually sinks in and takes root. You have the power to program your mind. You do it all the time and don't even know it. Be careful of how you speak to yourself. Your subconscious is always listening, and it will follow your command.

Inside Out

How you speak to yourself directly affects your outward communication to the people around you. The story we are telling ourselves about the situation we are in and about how we feel about ourselves always comes first, before any outward communication. If the inside voice is not calm and confident, the outside voice cannot be. Many people think that improving their speaking voice is just about increasing volume or speaking slower or deeper. And yes, that is all very important, as we'll learn in the next chapter. But we also have to learn to be in command of our inside voice. It's the voice of our spirit, the voice that allows us to trust ourself or not.

Three things can have a big impact on our inner voice of Calmfidence:

- Fear of mistakes
- A negative comfort zone
- Self-monitoring

FEAR OF MISTAKES

In chapter 2 we talked about a big Calmfidence killer: perfectionism. For over ten years I've been teaching weekly broadcasting and on-camera presentation classes in the Film Center Building in New York City. Having a location smack in the middle of the theater district makes for an incredible mix of students in each class, including Broadway performers, models, comedians, actors, broadcasters, executives, fashionistas, and even medical and financial professionals. It's a diverse bunch of people and a multicultural extravaganza of students from around the United States and around the world. God bless the Big Apple!

The one thing that many of my students have in common is that they worry about making a mistake in front of the group and in front of the camera. Being in the spotlight is a strange place. It's an island of contradiction. You are the focus, but you have to take the focus off of yourself. It never fails: once someone is afraid that they are going to mess up, they usually do. It's a self-fulfilling prophecy. They get stuck in their heads. They focus on themselves and not at the task at hand. They screw up, blank out, trip over their words, and forget what they were about to say.

When we focus on not wanting to make a mistake, on trying to be perfect, we are not focusing on the real job in front of us—making a connection with another human being. Whether it's through a camera lens, in front of an audience, or across a table in an interview, if we are coming from a place of worry, fear, doubt, or lack of trust in ourselves, the way these thoughts and feelings make us act is much worse than actually making the mistake. Living in fear of making a mistake is the mother of mistake-making. So, the first thing we work on is to not only expect mistakes but to count on them, to accept that they come with the territory.

Many times, when a student is presenting a script or telling a story in front of the camera, the golden moments happen when the mistakes happen. This is when we really get to see who they are. More personality kicks in. Instead of playing it safe, sounding like they are reading a script or overrehearsed, the unexpected moments let us see the human being again.

Think of your favorite television personalities or the public speakers you've enjoyed watching or listening to. I bet you don't mind when they make a flub or mistake here and there—this makes them more real, more approachable, and more human, more like us. Perfect people can be uncomfortable, even annoying to watch. They seem plastic and insincere; we don't relate to them. When it comes to public speaking, the audience actually forgets any mistakes you've made if they leave with something they can use. If you have given them something of value, something they can apply to their own lives, an idea, an inspiration, knowledge, or motivation, that is what they'll remember; that's all that will matter to them. A good rule of thumb when it comes to mistakes: if you don't mind, they don't mind!

Mistakes allow us to test the waters. They allow us to try things on for size. Learning how *not* to do something is just as important as learning how to do something. Relax, be human, be flexible, be real. Perfect is often fake and inaccessible. Be authentic with your imperfections and you *will* be good! To quote John Steinbeck from the movie based on his book *East of Eden*, "And now that you don't have to be perfect, you can be good."

I love when I see a client, performer, or public speaker flub, stumble, or make a mistake and just let it roll off their back. It's in those moments that we get to see their humanness. It makes them more like us, real human beings that we can relate to. Not some robotic, plastic, fake façade of a person. During my trainings and workshops it's in those imperfect moments where the magic happens if they roll with it, don't judge themselves, and just move on, either in a humorous way or in a matter-of-fact way. That is, if they roll with it, don't judge themselves, and just move on, either in a humorous way or in a matter-of-fact way. Most of the time people don't even notice imperfections unless you call attention to them by feeling awkward, apologizing, making excuses, or getting embarrassed. When you're dealing with an audience, the general rule of thumb is they don't care about a mistake unless the person making one does.

A NEGATIVE COMFORT ZONE

Anyone can lose Calmfidence when they are outside of their comfort zone in unfamiliar territory. It's hard to feel sure of yourself when you feel like a fish out of water or put in a position you would not choose to be in. But comfort zones are not necessarily positive places. Sometimes we are actually in a comfort zone when we believe negative things about ourselves.

For instance, if you were constantly told that you were stupid and that you didn't know what you were talking about, you may be negatively programmed subconsciously and not even realize it. If you believe that you are not good enough, don't deserve better, or are not valued, you can actually feel uncomfortable when you try to improve yourself or your life situation. When you try to do something good for yourself, it can actually feel wrong, not worth the discomfort, or crazy to even try.

If you are having trouble gaining a positive outlook, accepting yourself as valuable and deserving of love or success, go back in your mind and search for people and events that may have been the root of your negative beliefs. Decide from this point on that if you are outside of your comfort zone when you try to treat yourself well, change your life for the better, or believe in yourself, you will allow yourself to feel the discomfort and do it anyway. Don't let those awkward foreign feelings stop you. It's just like anything else: the more you do it, the easier it gets, and one success always builds on another. When a negative thought comes in, replace it with a positive one. Again, it's almost impossible to think a positive thought and a negative thought simultaneously. If there is one thing you have complete control over in your life, it is the thoughts you choose to think and choose to believe. It is up to you and only you.

SELF-MONITORING

When I first started coaching clients, I felt as though I were an impostor. I felt as though I was observing the client observing me! It felt a bit like an out-of-body experience. After I got a few sessions under my belt, I learned to trust my instincts and stop minimizing my training, background, and experience. This self-monitoring subsided as I found my comfort zone and a rhythm where I knew I could determine my clients' needs and help them. Self-monitoring combines a couple of the Calmfidence killers we discussed in chapter 2: the inner critic and excessive self-consciousness.

For the next twenty-four hours, notice how you speak to yourself. Is your self-talk positive or negative? Are you second guessing yourself? Pay attention to how your inner dialogue influences how you communicate outwardly to others.

Manage your inner voice of Calmfidence by:

- Speaking only in positive empowering terms to yourself. When you hear a negative statement come up in your self-talk, reframe it in a positive way as quickly as possible.

- Talking to yourself about what you want to go right, not what could go wrong.

- Identifying the negative comfort zones that you may have slipped into. Have you gotten comfortable believing a negative thing about yourself? Once you identify it, work to get out of that comfort zone even if it feels uncomfortable to do so.

- If you catch yourself self-monitoring, put up a mental stop sign in your mind's eye and switch gears to focus externally on what's happening around you.

Once you begin to control your inner voice of Calmfidence and start speaking to yourself in more positive, empowering ways, you'll find it much easier to be more calm and confident when you speak to other people. Remember that our outer voice stems from our inner voice. Which brings us to our next chapter: "The Outer Voice of Calmfidence."

A Client's Story

Hannah had a fear of communicating with others because she had trouble communicating with herself. Her self-talk was anxious and unhelpful: "I can't do this. I'm going to blank out. I'm going to sound stupid. What if they ask me something I don't have an answer for? What if the words won't come out of my mouth? Last time was a disaster. I couldn't even speak. I sounded like an idiot. I just want to run away. I hate myself for feeling this way." This was Hannah's self-talk leading up to any conference call or meeting at work. Then the physical part would kick in. Her heart would pound, she would feel dizzy, and she'd become an emotional wreck.

By Hannah's estimation, this was how she had talked to herself for the past twenty years. She had anxiety every day. It would start with her thoughts and snowball into a full-blown physical response as any communication with others approached. She would die a thousand deaths before the actual moment she was dreading. Hannah would procrastinate on preparing for any conversation, meeting, or presentation because even the preparation created anxiety as it made her visualize disaster and failure. This was both a vicious cycle and a self-fulfilling prophecy for Hannah.

When she came to me, the stakes were even higher than normal. "Well, I dug myself a really big hole with my new executive vice president when I was merely trying to introduce myself to her through email. Now she wants to set up a video meeting with me to learn about my role. I screwed myself by saying hello! My stomach is in knots and I want to cancel, but it's too late. I'm going to make a bad first impression. My role's not that important. I'm not good enough. She'll probably want to let me go from the team. My body and mind are a complete mess!" Actually, Hannah's new executive vice president simply wanted to have an introductory call to get to know her, but Hannah magnified the impact of the call into a life-or-death moment for her career.

After several weeks of phone sessions, Hannah and I developed a plan, and Hannah finally had a breakthrough. I asked Hannah to write down a list of all the things she liked about herself. Next I had her compile a list of all of her accomplishments at work, skills, and things she knew she was good at. We brainstormed three empowering words that she could coach herself with to keep her self-talk positive. When the time came to prepare for the big meeting, we scheduled an extra phone session to mentally prepare on an early Sunday morning. Hannah was stressing big time, and I could tell by her comments that she was going to put off writing her outline for Monday's call until Sunday night or possible even early Monday morning.

"How much calmer and more relaxed would you be if you could enjoy your Sunday and launch into Monday knowing you were finished with all of our preparation for this call, Hannah?" I asked.

"That would be amazing, but I know I'll find a lot of other things to do first today to try to avoid the anxiety," she responded.

"So right here, right now, Hannah, I'm staying on this call with you while you write your outline until you are done," I said. For the next hour and a half, we worked through everything she wanted to share with the vice president and answers to possible questions that might come up. This was the first time Hannah was prepared for a 10 o'clock Monday call at 10:30 a.m. on a Sunday morning. It felt good. She didn't spend the rest of her Sunday beating herself up because she was procrastinating. She was more relaxed when she fell asleep and was able to focus on what she wanted to have happen instead of fearing what might happen that next day. When she felt anxious, she reviewed her outline. When the inner critic kicked in, her inner coach said, "Follow your plan."

The call went well. "I can't believe I'm saying this," Hannah reported, "but the meeting went great today and my brain didn't freeze. The conversation flowed, and it started to feel a little more natural, less forced. It's so hard for me to see that I can actually do this, but it certainly went better than I expected." Hannah still had a lot more work to do to change twenty years of negative self-talk, but she had just gained some of the Calmfidence she needed.

Calmfidence Reflections

List three negative self-talk statements you make and how you could frame them more positively:

_____

_____

_____

List three things you feel may have become a negative comfort zone for you:

_____

_____

_____

10

The Outer Voice
of Calmfidence

When you've spent your whole life listening to others, it takes
courage to pay attention to the sound of your own voice.

Anonymous

It was Lilly's first big event as a health and wellness coach, promoting
her new book to a sea of blank faces in a packed ballroom. The wife of a
well-known TV personality, she was not yet known in her own right. She
just knew that everyone had come out to see the woman *he* was married
to, and she had convinced herself that she was riding on her husband's
coattails, even though she had so much of her own expertise to offer.

"Now if everyone could please just look at this slide for a minute, it
will show you an important way to pay attention to your health," Lilly
said in a hesitant monotone and barely audible voice that competed with
clinking silverware and growing chatter. The audience was not paying
attention to her or her presentation, and the microphone could not project her soft voice throughout the room. After about fifteen minutes, the
audience simply tired of struggling to hear her. It was like watching an
energy wave break across the room as table by table began turning into
their own circle of conversation and tuning out Lilly.

The evening had started out well when Lilly met with individual attendees as they lined up for her book signing. But when it was her time to take
the stage, the small voice in her throat and the small voice in her mind were

no match for that big audience in that big ballroom. She was dying up there, and I felt like I was one of the only people witnessing her fading away. Suddenly Lilly's assistant scurried onto the stage and whisked Lilly out the door. The audience didn't even realize that she had stopped talking. I shot across the room to follow Lilly down the hall to offer her my card.

Lilly and I worked hard for several months to dissect both her inside voice and outside voice. Lilly started to own her expertise and had stopped comparing herself and her goals to her husband and his fame. She stopped second guessing every word coming out of her mouth, was more in command of her self-talk, and now spoke with conviction, positivity, and enthusiasm. Her volume had increased as her confidence increased. She knew that she had something to say that was of great value to her audience. Lilly now commanded a room with her voice: "If you want to look and feel like a million bucks, here are five foods you should never eat again!" During her next presentation the audience was captivated by her voice of Calmfidence and eager to learn from her.

Your Body's Microphone

What does your voice say about you? Do people want to listen to you? Do you want to listen to yourself? We tell the world how we feel about ourselves by the way we use our voice. It is our body's microphone. Our voice is our own personal broadcast announcer. Are you soft-spoken? Is your tone high-pitched? Do you sound nasal or squeaky? Are you a fast or slow talker? Do you end up in "high C," your voice rising as you speak longer and get tenser, or do you swallow your words or mumble? You can learn how to use your personal microphone to be heard, to speak your mind, to stand up for what you believe in, to own the room.

How to Speak with Calmfidence

GET COMFORTABLE WITH THE SOUND OF YOUR OWN VOICE

I'm amazed when I hear people say they hate their voices. That's like saying they hate their vision or hate their hearing! We need to be aware of what we sound like to others so we can take charge and cultivate the voice that we want to project out into the world. Record yourself in private with either an audio recorder or a video recorder. Record both a normal conversation and a short little speech. Play it back over and over until your voice no longer sounds foreign to you.

SPEAK FROM YOUR BELLY

Many people speak from "up north"—from the nose (nasal talkers), the throat (high-pitched talkers), or the chest (low talkers). But when you pull up your words from your belly button, you get a powerful launching pad of sound that is fuller, deeper, richer, and projects much further.

Breathe from your belly. In chapter 6, "Calmfidence Tools," we learned about the Calmfidence breath tool, which we can use when we are stressed, nervous, or rushed. As we tend to take shallow breaths at these times, these shallow breaths make us sound stressed, nervous, and rushed. Watch a baby breathe and you'll see their whole tummy fill up like a balloon and deflate again. Most adults lose this ability, and that's really a shame because it calms you down, controls your heart rate, and helps you think more clearly. It also gives you a powerful voice that you are in full control of.

SPEAK UP IN LINE AT THE COFFEE SHOP

Start practicing speaking up loud and strong with a direct, pleasant, strong voice everywhere you go throughout the day. When you begin to do this in no-pressure situations, you can really test the waters and play with it. The more comfortable you get with this in your day-to-day interactions, the more natural it will feel to be in charge of your voice in high-pressure situations like giving a speech, going on an interview, dealing with confrontation, and negotiating for what you want. You will trust the voice coming out of your mouth. You will know its power, and how to use it.

TALK TO THE BACK OF THE ROOM WHEN YOU ARE IN FRONT OF A GROUP

If you focus on making sure that the people who are the furthest away from you can hear you, then you'll be sure that everyone in the room can hear you loud and clear. Don't make people struggle to have to hear you. They don't want to have to work that hard and they will tune you out.

DON'T EAT, SWALLOW, OR MUMBLE YOUR WORDS

If you are going to open up your mouth to say something, fully commit! A national television network asked me to work with one of its hosts who was talking too low when he would interject comments into his entertainment news reports. He had a comedic background and would sprinkle in some very clever and funny comments, but when he did so he said those bits more softly than the rest of his news. He was throwing them away as he said them. Many times, viewers would miss what he actually said, and so would the producers. It was driving them crazy.

After working with him, I realized he was not 100 percent sure of his comments. He was on the fence on whether they were actually funny enough, so he did not send them out fully. He did not own them. He wasn't all in. When people second-guess themselves like this, their voice gives them away.

There is no way to please all the people all the time with your point of view, personal sense of humor, or observations, and that's okay. You have to find a way to be satisfied with your own outlook on things and be willing to send it out there fully, whether everyone laughs or not, or agrees with you or not. Stand up for our own judgment calls. People tend to follow the lead of others who know where they are going. This goes for your conversations, presentations, commentary, and belief in your own opinion.

ENJOY THE SOUND OF YOUR VOICE

Once you get to know your voice, you can begin to like your voice—and even love your voice. It's like getting in touch with your body in much the same way that someone does when doing yoga, working out, stretching, controlling their breathing, or meditating. When you are in tune with your body, you can appreciate its health, its beauty, its capabilities. The same goes for your voice. When you work to get in tune with this awesome communication device, you can cultivate it, master it, and use it in many wonderful ways.

FIND YOUR VOCAL S-P-I-R-I-T

Passion is the spark that lights up the effectiveness of a public speaker, but feeling passionate and sounding passionate are two very different things. What it really comes down to is energy. It's about the vibe, the feeling, and the life behind your words. You've got to connect with your vocal S-P-I-R-I-T:

S—Selflessness: When you speak to a group, to an individual, or to a camera, you have to be selfless. It has to be more about those on the receiving end and less about you. In the laugh.com comedy recording series *Jerry Seinfeld on Comedy*, the comedian is asked how he finds confidence on the stage while doing his stand-up routines. He said that it all comes down to really liking the audience. He said, "Find a way to love those people out there." Aim for a way to be among them, to be one of them. I have found it's about being of service, having the intention of giving away something of value that they can benefit from.

P—Passion: Have a strong belief in what you are talking about. Enthusiasm is contagious and motivating. If you are not convinced about what you are saying, it will be absolutely impossible to convince anyone else.

I—Interest: Have a genuine interest in the person or people you are talking to. Many people just go through the motions for a paycheck, an obligation, or to be courteous. Cultivate a genuine interest in the people you are communicating with.

R—Relate: Do you know enough about the audience or person you are speaking with to be able to relate to them? Do you know their needs? Do you know about their experiences? If you can't relate to them, they will not relate to you.

I—Intention: Have a strong desire to educate, entertain, inform, inspire, motivate, or put others at ease.

T—Trust: Not only do you have to work hard to earn the trust of the individual or audience you are speaking to, you also have to trust yourself. You have to learn to trust the voice in your head so that you can trust the voice coming out of your mouth.

INCREASE YOUR VOCAL D-E-P-T-H

D—Be Direct: Have a point and get to the point. Think things through and speak in a definite manner—one that shows that you know what your point of view is, you know what you want to say, and you know the end result you are looking for. Tell it like it is. Be clear, concise, and don't beat around the bush.

E—Be Engaging: Really be present and in the moment when you speak with another person. Make it your goal to be understood and to understand. Make it your goal to connect with the person you are speaking with, build rapport, and find common ground.

P—Control Your Pitch: Be conscious of the pitch of your voice; seek to speak in a deeper, pleasant pitch free of whiny, shrieking tones.

T—Adjust Your Tempo: Speed is an indicator of nerves. Fast talkers are perceived as being nervous or trying to get something over on someone. Some people don't seem to come up for air. We can't digest what they are saying. Think of your voice as a musical instrument. A frantic tempo sets a very definite tone, as does an easy-going tempo.

H—Be Human: Seek to speak in an accessible, real, conversational manner.

LOWER YOUR REGISTER

Often when we speak, we tend to get up into a higher pitch as we go along. This is especially true if we are stressed, emotional, in a rush, or trying to fit in too much information in a short amount of time. When we make a conscious effort to lower the depth of our voice, we sound more composed and trustworthy. A strategy that works well is to bring down your voice each time you start a new sentence. This is even more effective for women, who tend to end up in high C as their speech or conversation progresses.

A close friend of mine, a vocal coach who worked on Broadway, recommends saying the word *mood* over and over again to help control the depth of your voice. You may start to feel like you sound like a cow, but it works. As you pronounce *mood*, you will feel your stomach muscles engage and feel the word coming up from a lower place down the back of your throat. It will open up the back of your throat and help open a pathway to get to your belly.

INCREASE YOUR VOLUME

You will actually appear less nervous to others when you speak with a volume that is loud and clear. When you keep putting off speaking up, it will get harder and harder to open your mouth.

When I teach group classes, everyone in the group knows that eventually it will be their turn to get up and speak in front of the room. Yet when I call for volunteers you can hear crickets. I explain to them that the longer they wait, the harder it will get. Anxiety will build. Self-doubt will build. I like to pull out full water bottles and ask them each to hold one with their arm extended. At first, it's easy. After all, a water bottle doesn't weigh very much, but after a couple minutes that bottle begins to get heavy, very heavy. After more than a few minutes it might as well be a hundred-pound barbell. I explain to them that this is what happens psychologically when they put off getting up in front of the room. They end up paralyzed or weighed down with anxiety.

MOVE IT!

The way you use your body has a huge impact on your voice. In my performance career I have had the opportunity to do narration for commercials, movies, and television programs. As my fellow voice-over performers will attest, it's always better to stand up while doing this type of recording. In voice-over narration, it's important to use your body and hand gestures to help tell a story, to help create the right energy, and to help your breathing.

When we sit or slouch, our diaphragms literally crunch our voices. Crunching is that place in your torso where you do a physical crunch for a sit-up exercise. When I coach my clients to be their best during telephone interviews, I always recommend that they stand rather than sit, so they have a more dynamic energy, stay fully present in the moment, and have a stronger vocal quality.

Even the way you dress your body will affect your voice. Your voice will sound different during a phone interview when you are in sweat-pants or PJs than when you are dressed in a suit or other professional attire. Your clothing affects your attitude and your energy. The way you carry your body or "block" off your body also influences your ability to use your voice to its fullest potential.

When I work with television clients who stand up while presenting on camera, their voices are less effective when they cross their arms, clasp their hands, or stuff their hands inside their pockets. People need hand gestures to help get the words out and to help them flow. You can even hear the difference and feel a different energy when someone crosses their ankles or arms while standing or if they start pacing or rocking in place.

When you want to make a great impression, aim for these three vocal *P*'s:

- Be pleasant.
- Be personable.
- Be passionate.

To be an effective communicator, avoid these vocal turn-offs:

- Speaking too softly.
- Speaking in a monotone voice.
- Speaking in a high-pitched voice with a squeaky vocal quality.
- Mumbling.
- Speaking out of the side of your mouth.
- Speaking in a sing-song manner.
- Fast talking.
- Loud talking.
- Sounding whiny.
- Nasal tone.
- Speaking through your teeth.
- Blurting out words without thinking.
- Using filler words such as um, uh, ya know, er, and like (we'll dive deeper into this in chapter 14, "Public-Speaking Calmfidence").
- Using filler phrases like "to be honest" and "actually."

STEER CLEAR OF THE THROAT CLEAR!

There are many things that make you feel like you have to clear your throat. But when it comes to speaking in public, on camera, during a meeting, or over the phone, throat clearing can send the wrong message, making you sound nervous, unsure, unprepared, and even untrustworthy.

The top throat-clearing culprits are:

- Allergies
- Dairy
- Food
- Caffeine
- Stress/anxiety
- Dehydration
- Acid reflux
- Smoking
- Voice strain
- Cold/virus
- Habit

If any if these are your throat-clearing triggers, take extra steps before your next speech or meeting to be sure to:

- Take allergy or cold medicine as needed.
- Hydrate.
- Avoid dairy.
- Limit caffeine.
- Brush your tongue.
- Take an antacid.
- Avoid eating close to the event or meeting.
- Avoid smoking prior to your talk
- Pamper your voice.
- Clear your throat in private just prior to your talk.
- Suck on lozenges before you start your talk.
- Carry extra water with you.

Telephone Calmfidence

Communicating with Calmfidence over the phone is more important than ever. When you're on the phone other people can't see you, unless of course you are on a video call. They can't make any decisions or conclusions about you except for how you use your voice. Many times, a phone call may be your first contact with someone you will later meet in person, but right now your voice is all they've got to go on. It's an important first impression that can set the tone for your in-person meeting later. The great thing about speaking with someone via the phone is that you actually have a lot more control over the situation than you would face-to-face. Following are some things you can do to communicate with Calmfidence on the phone.

MAKE SURE TO MINIMIZE BACKGROUND NOISE

Nothing is more distracting to both you and the person on the other end of the phone than loud or odd noises going on around you. When you know your call is important, take it to another room. Move away from other people, machine noise, loudspeakers, intercoms, traffic noise, babies, kids, dogs, or jack hammers! Don't make an important call if you can't control the background noise.

TIMING IS EVERYTHING

Try to determine what the person receiving your call is doing and when. Monday mornings, lunch hours, and the end of the day are not generally the best time to call someone. However, calling an executive before or after work hours is often a good time as many productive people get in early and leave late and will not be distracted by a busy office in the background.

CREATE A PLAN

Decide, plan, and commit to a solid opening line and at least two closing line options, depending on the desired outcome of the call. There's nothing worse than teetering between a few possible opening lines once your answerer picks up and says hello. Have you ever stumbled over your words by blending two different opening statements together because you didn't commit to one and stick with it? This is a very common cause of getting tongue-tied. Decide on one line and stick with it.

If your call falls in the category of confrontational, uncomfortable, or dreaded, write out a script. Plan exactly what you want to say and how you want to say it. Write it out fully and then turn it into bullet points in the order you want to cover them. This will give you a solid framework to follow without sounding like you're reading off a piece of paper.

BE DEFINITE

End your sentences so they sound like you have ended your point. Don't go up in your inflection at the end of sentences (called *upspeaking*) or your statements will sound more like questions, and you will sound unsure of yourself.

DON'T BE AFRAID OF SILENCE ONCE YOU HAVE COMPLETED A STATEMENT

Speak your piece, ask your question, or state your request, problem, or solution, and then simply wait for the other person to give their response. Do not be compelled to fill in the dead air if they do not respond immediately. Doing so will make you stumble to find additional words, and you will sound as if you have the need to justify what you just said, or you will seem to not be giving the other person time to think about what you just said. A few seconds may feel like an eternity, but it really isn't.

DON'T BE A DEAD RINGER

It only takes about three seconds for someone to size you up over the phone, and they can't even see you! Wow, we better get this one right. The other day I heard my husband on the phone in his office trying to get something worked out with an insurance company. After the first call, he hung up the phone and said, "Drip." After the second call, he hung up the phone and said, "Wow, what a great lady; she really had her act together."

I asked him why he called the first person a drip. He said, first it sounded like the guy had marbles in his mouth. He was talking so quietly he could hardly be heard, and he pretty much sounded like he was at death's door. The second person was an energetic woman who said if she couldn't help, she'd be sure to find someone who could. She was upbeat and alive and seemed genuinely interested in helping. Gee, I wonder which one of them will be moving up in that company!

Every time I call a particular friend, she sounds as if she is suffering from some illness when she answers the phone. This makes me ask her, "What's wrong?" She replies, "Nothing," and then perks up. I can't figure this one out. She doesn't realize what a downer it is to call her and hear that tone in her voice, and I'm her friend! What must a stranger's first impression be?

Voice-overs are narrations that you hear actors doing in commercials, audiobooks, and documentaries where you don't see the performer—you only hear their voice. When I first trained to do voice-overs myself, I couldn't believe how much facial expression and body movement I needed to muster up to bring the voice-overs to life. It's the same for people who work on radio; they need to create images with their voice, energy, and storytelling skills. Well, it's the same on the phone.

When you smile when you're talking on the phone, it changes your whole delivery and tone, and if you are sitting there like a lump you'll sound like a lump. If you're answering a phone for your job, your own company, or even at home, the way you answer sets the tone for that phone call and for how people feel about you or that company. If you're not ready to deal with a particular call, then let the caller leave a voicemail and call that person back when you're ready to handle the phone call well.

We all have to make phone calls to try to get what we want. Whether it's a pizza delivered, an extension on credit, ordering room service, or calling the cable company, making the person on the other end of that phone want to help you is as easy as being upbeat, pleasant to deal with, knowing what you want, and sounding thankful for their help. It's really not that complicated, but so many people come off sounding like a drip . . . and no one is that motivated to help a drip!

VOICEMAIL CALMFIDENCE

Voicemail, both in the way you leave a message for someone else and how your outgoing message sounds to others, speaks volumes about you.

I had a client who wanted to break away from the marketing company he had worked at for years to start his own firm. He came to me to build up his communication skills and Calmfidence so that he would be able to handle all the challenges that came with going out on his own. I knew he could do it, because he was the backbone and the go-to guy already at his current job. After much planning and positioning, he did start his own company, and things were falling into place. One afternoon I called him to check in and I got his voicemail. As I listened to his outgoing message I was struck by how lackluster, monotone, and unappealing his voice was. I knew this guy well and I knew he was a good guy, a guy who could get the job done. He was a positive, solution-oriented person, but you would never know it by the sound of his voice. What a terrible first impression this would make to a stranger calling his company for the first time.

I spoke to him about it and told him to change that message right away to a more cheerful, bright, helpful-sounding tone. He did change it, and it was like listening to a different person. He sounded upbeat, dynamic, and positive. He realized how different it sounded—and others commented on the change. Not surprisingly, business seemed to pick up soon afterward.

I've worked with many young clients who just graduated from college and advised them to change their outgoing voicemail message to sound more professional and dynamic. Many had the old college party/hookup voice that sounded silly and immature. When recruiters and employers call the number on the top of their résumé, the voicemail needs to match up with the potential job candidate they have on the paper in front of them. This is also true for email addresses. Keep them professional. Avoid silly nicknames. These are small things that make a big difference.

Getting and Keeping the Floor

Do you have something to say? Does your heart pound just thinking about jumping into the conversation at work, the PTA meeting, or family gathering? Do you wait so long for the right moment that it never comes and the conversation has moved on past the point you wanted to make? Here are some tips that will help give you more Calmfidence to speak up, own your point of view, and trust that what you have to say is of value:

- Stop waiting for an invitation! Many people figure if you have something to say you will say it. If you wait for a formal invitation or prompting, it may never come.

- Don't be a victim of unintentional domination! Strong personalities, extroverts, people who love to hear themselves talk, or just plain excited enthusiasts often don't even realize they are dominating a conversation. They may not realize you are waiting for an opening or a lull so you can have a turn.

- Go ahead and jump! Close your eyes if you have to, but jump in! When you have something to say, open your mouth and speak loudly and clearly.

- Please interrupt! You can pleasantly and professionally interrupt and should interrupt if what you have to say is appropriate and relevant to the conversation.

- Make your mark. Put your hand up, stand up, place an object on the table, or touch the arm of the person who is talking.

- Challenge interruptions. If someone interrupts you once you finally muster the nerve to speak, don't let them. Say "please let me finish." Or use one of your markers by touching their arm again or hold your hand up like a crossing guard to an oncoming car. Pleasantly and professionally, yet firm.

- Remember: ideas are needed. If you've got one, send it out there loud and clear.

- Avoid using disempowering language such as "I could be wrong but," "Correct me if I'm wrong," "I'm not exactly an expert at this but," "Maybe this is just my opinion but," and "I don't want to step on any toes here but. . . ." All of these opening lines start you off from a negative place. It will sound like you assume or expect that others will receive what you have to say in a bad way. Launching into your input in this way minimizes what you have to say. This can be a habit for people who are simply trying to avoid sounding like a know-it-all, but these phrases take away your power and confident presence. Use these phrases instead: "I'd like to hear your thoughts on this," "Try this on for size," "What do you think of this idea?," "From my perspective it seems," and "Based on the facts I have I think. . ." These will make you sound more collaborative, open-minded, and confident.

When you know how to use your voice to express yourself and command attention, your credibility increases dramatically. Your voice will be one of the indicators of your level of calm and confidence. When you work to improve your vocal qualities, eliminate bad habits, and begin to enjoy the way you are able to use your voice to connect and communicate with others, you will be much more likely to speak up for yourself and even for those around you who may not be able to speak up for themselves. When you have the voice of Calmfidence, people know it.

In the next chapter, we'll move to a related topic in our exploration of communication Calmfidence: "The Eyes of Calmfidence."

Calmfidence Reflections

List three things you like about the sound of your voice:

_____

_____

_____

List three ways you can find your vocal S-P-I-R-I-T:

_____

_____

_____

List three ways you can improve your vocal D-E-P-T-H:

_____

_____

_____

List any vocal turn-offs or bad habits that you want to improve on or eliminate:

_____

_____

_____

List three ways you will speak up and have your voice be heard:

_____

_____

_____

11

The Eyes of Calmfidence

Looking into someone's eyes
changes the entire conversation.
Kushandwizdom

E ye contact is an intimate thing. People might really see us for who we are: it can make us feel vulnerable, as if they are looking into our soul. If we don't have the eyes of Calmfidence, that can be hard to take. Eye contact improves when:

- You trust yourself.
- You know what you want to say.
- You know what you want.
- You are comfortable with yourself and therefore more comfortable with others.
- You think more about the other person and worry less about yourself.
- You are engaged and really listening in the moment.
- You get desensitized to eye contact.

When Honesty's Too Much

Direct eye contact is sometimes just too much for some people. They have to build up to it over time. You can practice making better eye contact by:

- Looking in the mirror and making eye contact with your own image.

- Watching YouTube videos and using apps that are designed for eye-contact practice.

- Gazing into the eyes of people in advertising photos, social media, or images on the web.

- Practicing with people you love and trust. Videotape your practice and watch yourself.

- Practicing with strangers in low-stake situations where the outcome isn't highly important to you, like interacting with a cashier, coffee barista, dry cleaner, or a person younger than you.

- Making a game out of it for yourself. See if you can connect eyes for just a bit longer each time you look at someone.

- Trying short bursts of eye contact when saying hello and goodbye to people.

If you catch yourself avoiding eye contact:

- Ask yourself, "Why do I feel uncomfortable right now?"

- Ask, "Am I uncomfortable about how I feel about this person, or how I feel about myself?"

- Commit to actively listening and really trying to understand what the other person is saying. Try to let go of thinking about yourself at all.

- Know that you do not have to maintain direct eye contact the whole time. It's normal to look inward, up, or to the side to recall information or to digest what the other person is saying.

- Scan the other person's face. Look at each eye, then the eyebrows, the nose, and the mouth.

- Scanning the face shows you are actively listening and gathering meaning from the person's nonverbal cues.

- Nod and tilt your head to show you understand what they are saying and that you are fully present in the moment with them.

- Keep your chin up so that it's harder for you to look down and away.

Meaningful Eye Contact

Eye contact, or the absence of it, tells people volumes about how we feel about them and how we feel about ourselves. When we can look at another person directly in the eyes and really connect with them, we get the opportunity to build trust and understanding. When we don't look people in the eye, there is a real disconnect.

Meaningful eye contact happens when we make a real effort to see the other person. We're not just looking at them, but we are seeing them. This difference makes people feel important, relevant, and respected. They feel that they are our main focus, our priority, that nothing else matters more than connecting with them at that moment.

When we make meaningful eye contact, we are also letting others see us.

- We are letting them in.

- We are seen as approachable, accessible, and real.

- It's no longer a surface interaction, a façade, or a guarded communication.

Of course, this all makes sense only when it is our intention to truly connect with people and be a better communicator. There are times when we simply cannot allow others this kind of access. Unfortunately, many people operate in an evasive mode all the time as a protection mechanism, and they miss out on so much because of it.

Eye Contact Turn-Offs

THE STALKER STARE

Meaningful eye contact can get pretty intense if we overdo it. Be sure to avoid the "stalker stare." A laser focus into another person's eyes can only feel comfortable for short periods of time, and then both people need a break. When we process information or think through our thoughts, we need to look into our mind's eye, which makes us look up or down as we scan our minds. This is normal and expected. When someone doesn't do this and maintains a straight gaze at us, it will begin to feel confrontational or creepy. Be sure to look away to ponder, to consider, to think things over so you can break up that direct eye contact a bit. A good gauge of time is two to five seconds. Maintaining eye contact for two to five seconds at a time feels comfortable to both parties. Less than two seconds feels like a quick getaway, and longer than five seconds starts to feel too long.

The stalker stare does serve a purpose, however. You can use it to hold your ground, to let someone know you mean business. It can be used to intimidate, manipulate, and throw people off their game. If that's not your intention, be careful. The stalker stare can also lead people to believe you are a little bonkers.

I was once hired to coach a very intense and brilliant musician. He needed to learn to be able to read a teleprompter for an upcoming television entertainment event he would be hosting. He really didn't want to come to the coaching session. His people felt like he needed to be coached more than he did. He came into our meeting unwillingly and proceeded to sit down directly across from me and locked his dark eyes on me with such intensity that he didn't even blink. He wasn't interested in building rapport or making this session easy on me in any way. He was deliberately being a tough case and he did it all with just his eyes, which said, "Show me what you got and let's get this over with."

His intense prolonged eye contact threw me for a moment. It even crossed my mind that he might be unstable or on something. I didn't retreat. I decided to focus on the job I was hired to do. He needed help, and I knew that I knew my stuff, so I just did my thing. I ignored what he was doing and made my own comfortable eye contact anyway. I talked to him with civility, one person to another, even though he was not treating me civilly. I showed him how he could perform better in front of a camera. Slowly his icy eyes thawed, he began to mirror my communication, and when our session finally came to an end, he actually gave me a hug before leaving the training room.

THE DART BOARD

When a person's eyes frequently dart to the left and the right it almost always means something is up. When I coach people to look directly into the camera, I tell them it's okay to glance up and down a bit. But if they glance left or right on camera, they immediately look nervous, unsure, uncomfortable, or aware of other people in the room. This is true when a person is not in front of a camera, too. Shifty eyes make you look, well, shifty—evasive, untrustworthy, and dishonest. Eye darting means you are focused on something else, not the person you are talking to. So, try not to throw darts when you talk to people!

THE EYEBALL LOCK

There are some people who believe that it's best to just pick one eye and look into it when talking to someone. I don't get this. If you start looking at one eyeball, you've stopped looking at the person! I need to keep things moving and scan around the person's face for clues and connections. If I stare into one eyeball, well then, I'm communicating with an eyeball; it may as well be sitting on a plate. We need to scan others' facial expressions for cues and nuances. Notice eyebrows, the nose, the mouth, and the general look of the entire face. Take it all in to create a big picture of what the other person is thinking and feeling. As you scan their face along with both eyes, you will be getting the maximum amount of information, and you will appear engaged and likeable without making them or yourself feel awkward or uncomfortable.

VIP EYE CONTACT

Have you ever been talking to someone at a party and you notice them scanning the room to see who else is there? Their eyes are basically telling you that they're just talking to you until they find somebody better to talk to. This is a big mistake that a lot of people make, especially at networking events. Truly great communicators operate in tight, moment-by-moment compartments. They have the ability to make the one person they are talking to feel like the most important person in that room. Like anything else, it's quality, not quantity. If you can be truly present, fully, for just a few moments with just one person, you will actually have more time to connect with additional people throughout a room, and they will all feel like you acknowledged them and gave a damn.

SELECTIVE EYE CONTACT

Not long ago I went shopping for a new car with my husband. When we met with the salesman, even though we told him I was the one who would be purchasing the car, he continued to selectively make eye contact with just my husband. This was infuriating. Maybe he was more comfortable talking guy talk with another guy, or he didn't want to come across as if he was giving me all the attention (my husband is 6'4" and can be a bit intimidating just by his size alone), but whatever the reason, it told me that this salesman was not a good salesman. He didn't get the fact that if he couldn't address me directly, he should have at least split his eye contact equally between us. This should just be common sense. Because he didn't include both of us in his eye contact, I didn't like him. He lost my trust and he lost the sale.

Withholding eye contact is a strategy as well. It can make the other person feel less important, that you are not giving them your full attention or that you are freezing them out. This is even true in bird populations. For many years my husband and I had a pet blue-and-gold macaw parrot named Zackary. We worked with a bird trainer who had worked with the famous cockatoo in the 1970s TV drama *Baretta*. She told us that whenever Zackary did something that we did not want him to do, like bite or scream, we were to approach the cage and then turn our back to him with our shoulders up in a bit of a shrug. Apparently, this is what parrots in the wild do to reprimand each other or show disapproval. It actually worked!

So much of the work that I do with my clients involves creating a connection. When I coach people to appear on television and talk to viewers directly through the camera, all kinds of strange things happen at first. People don't know where to look. Their eyes dart around and bug out. Or they get a lifeless look in their eyes. When they first try to read a teleprompter, their eyes often lose all emotion and they get a robotic windshield wiper scanning motion in them.

This all happens because they're trying to communicate with a hunk of metal instead of a person. They're just staring into the black hole of the camera lens or reading white words scrolling hypnotically across a black screen. There's no human connection being made at all. The eyes tell us this immediately. Once I get clients to visualize a person they are talking to, to see them through the lens, past the teleprompter and in their environment listening to them, things start to change. It's got to be a one-on-one conversation with another human being. Think about what the look on your face might be if you imagine you are presenting to an inanimate object or a faceless mass of strangers. How different would that look be if you imagine you are having a conversation with a friend? Big difference. Once people get this, I've seen that look transform right before my eyes.

It's a similar situation when I coach people for public speaking. When a speaker is in a room full of people or on a stage staring at a sea of people, they get that same blank look in the eye when they're just seeing the audience as a group. Once they work on really connecting with individual human eyes around the room, things change big time. This connection can be scary at first. People feel vulnerable and exposed.

HIGH-TECH EYE PROBLEMS

Technology steals so much eye contact these days. The first time I noticed this, I was traveling around the country with a public relations executive who was overseeing a national media tour I was a spokesperson for. We didn't really know each other, but we got along fine, and sharing meals and cab rides was our opportunity to get to know each other better.

Then came the high-tech eye problems. Every time we would sit down to eat in a restaurant, this person could not keep her eyes off her phone. She was constantly checking her emails and voicemails during our conversations. Basically, I was sitting with a person yet eating alone. She couldn't even get through an hour-long meal without her attention going elsewhere. It was awkward and rude. Maybe she wasn't that interested in me or in the tour, but a good PR person should be able to fake it for just a little while.

Anything that takes your eyes away from another person's face, other than thinking and contemplating what they've said, is not a good thing. Constant checking of a cell phone, looking at a computer screen, checking out the fact that you could really use a manicure, picking lint off your jacket, or doing just about anything else that does not apply to the conversation tells the other person that you're just not that into them or you'd really rather be someplace else. While that might be true, it's simply not smart communication and it's not polite. People will always remember how you made them feel. If you can make everyone you talk to feel like the most important person in the room for just a few moments, you will build an army of people who appreciate you and the time you give them.

TUNED OUT

In the May 2013 *Wall Street Journal* article "The Decline of Eye Contact," Sue Shellenbarger wrote that lack of eye contact was becoming a big problem with technology, remote work environments, and multitasking. It's a huge problem in all levels of schooling, with remote learning and with students on their phones when they are in school instead of paying attention to teachers. It's also rude.

Unfortunately, it's becoming socially acceptable among different generations for people to continually check in with their phone so they don't miss anything, or if they're bored and looking for other social stimulation.

People are constantly checking their personal technology devices to see texts, social media, news and sports, shopping, photos, and other distractions. It's like the parents who used to videotape every minute of their child's events or parties but weren't fully present in the moment because they were too busy documenting it.

With today's preponderance of remote work environments, people are missing out on eye contact. Even during virtual meetings and presentations, it's still not direct eye contact—people are struggling to look between the lens and the faces on the screen. Talk about a barrier to real connection.

A study published in *Computers in Human Behavior* showed that young people who were dissatisfied with their lives or relationships were more likely to check their cell phones to see what they might be missing, whether during meals or other quality time with friends and family.

Younger generations are not always being taught the importance of eye contact. The best communicators know that they need to adapt and change around different people. When a twenty-something interacts with a forty- or fifty-something, they may not realize that technology distractions are not considered as acceptable as they are by their peers, and they may be seen as rude, immature, and lacking social savvy. People who are leaders or who are in charge tend to make longer eye contact than those who are not.

The ways you behave in your personal relationships may not translate to your professional relationships. Maybe your friends and family don't care if you check your phone when you're hanging out with them, but at work it's a whole different ball game, especially if you work with a mix of generations.

For instance, during a two-hour session with a client, I feel like I shouldn't check my phone at all since they are paying for two full hours of my attention. If there is something that I absolutely feel I have to check on during that time I will only do it while they are reading over a script or notes before they do their presentation or performance to camera. I want to be sure I'm only doing something else for myself if they are busy and do not require my attention for the moment. I even hesitate to do this, however, because I risk the possibility of thinking about what I just read or saw on my phone when I need to be fully in the moment with the client. I also try not to check my phone when I am helping my son with his homework or spending time with him during our personal time.

Healthy Eye Contact

Humans need contact. Our eyes influence the meaning of our words as much as the inflections of our voice delivering those words can change their meaning. I want you to try an experiment. Do not make eye contact with anyone at any time for one day. Try it. Wherever you go and whatever you do, no eye contact, with anyone anywhere. You'll start to feel like you're the last person on Earth. You'll start to feel a bit stressed out and less sure of yourself. Try this experiment just one day; I'll bet you can't make it through a full twenty-four hours. It's the opposite of a staring contest but harder because it starts to affect how you feel about yourself.

According to Quantified Impressions, a communications analytics company based in Texas, in the typical adult conversation people make eye contact 30–60 percent of the time, but 60–70 percent of the conversation should have eye contact in order to create an emotional connection. Since most of our decisions are based on emotions, this is a big disconnect. Just like a hug or physical contact, eye contact is important for emotional health. Humans thrive on connecting—feeling like they are seen and heard. We have five senses for a reason.

Children may not always make good eye contact. This might be because they are immature, shy, nervous, distracted, or haven't been taught that it's part of good manners and respectful attention skills. But when they are on the receiving end of things, they surely seem to know they do not have an adult's full attention when the adult is not looking at them. My husband and I worked hard to teach our son the importance of making eye contact with adults and teachers. Of course, we would glow when we would get feedback from people on how well he would engage while many others his age did not. Then one day our son gave me a taste of my own medicine when he was trying to talk to me as I was working on my laptop. I answered him with an "I'm listening" as I continued to work. He said, "No, Mom, listen with your eyes!" Boy, did that floor me. He was right. I wasn't giving him my full attention and he called me out on it.

EQUAL OPPORTUNITY EYE CONTACT

Making eye contact with everyone who is listening to you, especially in a group, is key. It doesn't matter if you are giving a presentation or speech to ten people or a thousand people, each person wants to feel like you are talking just to them. Think about it. An audience is not receiving your message as a group. Each member of the audience is listening and absorbing as an individual, as one person considering what your message means to them and their work or their life. So, when speaking to a room or group, don't leave people out! Speak to one person for a little while and then look over to another person and chat with them for a little while, and so on. This will do many things: it will help you connect with the audience better, they will feel you are really talking to them rather than at them, and you will suddenly feel that you are no longer under a big spotlight or microscope just speaking to a massive group of strangers.

When I teach my group classes, I understand that twelve to fifteen people are trying to get the most out of the session in the two hours we have together each week. Keep in mind that I also teach a tremendous amount of two-hour one-on-one sessions to private clients. The whole two hours gets to be intensely focused just on them and their needs. This just isn't possible in a group setting. So, I try to simulate this individual attention the best way I can: by connecting with each person in the group and giving them direct eye contact one person at a time during my lecture portion and then after each exercise. I make it my goal to give each participant equal time, equal attention, and equal eye contact. Those who don't have the biggest, boldest personalities in the room really appreciate this. (Many teachers give more attention to their outgoing students.)

Now that we've got our eyes on Calmfidence, it's time to learn about how we can have more confidence communicating with our facial nonverbal skills—bringing us to the next chapter on our journey: "Facing Calmfidence."

Knowing how to use your eyes with Calmfidence increases your calm communication skills by:

- Contributing to emotional health and keeping you fully present in the moment.

- Making you and those around you feel comfortable and at ease, building trust.

Knowing how to use your eyes with Calmfidence increases your confident communication skills by:

- Making you appear more confident to others.

- Showing others that they have your full attention, interest, and respect.

A Client's Story

"I just don't know where to look when I'm talking to some-one. I hate to admit it but it almost makes me feel naked. When I look into another person's eyes, I feel awkward and nervous," Carl said. He had always been uncomfortable making eye contact with people. He never liked being in the spotlight and was not one to make small talk easily. Now it was affecting his business relationships. Some cowork-ers thought he was arrogant and too self-important to give them his full attention. Others thought he was not truthful or trustworthy. Poor Carl was none of that. He felt just the opposite: vulnerable, anxious, and uncertain of his ability to communicate and connect with people. Carl was very good at his job—when he was behind closed doors . . . alone. His work was so good that he was on track to becoming a partner in his firm, but his inability to make eye contact was causing the other partners to hesitate to confirm him. The other partners constantly told Carl to "just look people in the eyes." But it wasn't that easy. Carl needed help.

"I had no idea I looked like that," Carl said when I played back the video that I had made of him talking so he could see for himself how he was coming across to others. "I look so uninterested, and I also look painfully nervous." After Carl practiced a few of our eye-contact exercises, I taped him again and reviewed the video with him to track his progress. It took several weeks of intense sessions practicing eye contact and viewing the images so that he could see how much more confident he looked even when he was feeling uncomfortable. Once those images sank in through repeated positive reinforcement, Carl could not deny that working on longer and better eye contact really made him a better communicator. And it made others more comfortable to be around him. As he implemented these exercises into real office situations, he started to notice a change, not just in his confidence but also in the way his coworkers responded to him more positively. A few months later, Carl made partner. He also gave himself a promotion to a new level of Calmfidence.

Calmfidence Reflections

List three ways that eye contact can make you feel uncomfortable, and why:

_____

_____

_____

List three ways you avoid making eye contact :

_____

_____

_____

How can you make eye contact feel less about you and more about connecting with others?

_____

_____

_____

12

Facing
Calmfidence

The face is the mirror of the mind, and eyes without
speaking confess the secrets of the heart.

St. Jerome

Smiling is a sign of weakness," Lewis said as we sat around the big gray conference table. Stone-faced and serious during his presentations, he would not crack a smile and lighten up in his session with me, either. I had been hired by a large glass manufacturer in Detroit to coach a group of their salespeople for presentation and communication skills. Throughout the morning, I had each participant come to the front of the room and deliver the sales presentation they had been giving to potential customers. I videotaped them, played back the videos to the group, suggested adjustments, and had them present again.

As the training day went on, everyone made great progress—except for Lewis. "Try smiling at the beginning and the end of your presentation, Lewis," I suggested. Lewis maintained his serious face.

"Smiling when you are offering solutions and the benefits of your products is always a great idea, Lewis," I said. In response, Lewis "softened" from serious to stern face.

As we gathered around the conference table for our lunch break, we discussed everyone's progress for the first part of the day. When I made my way around the table to Lewis, he revealed that he was a retired US Marine.

"I want to have credibility and for people to take me seriously. I don't have time for silliness," he said. Lewis knew the industry better than the rest of his sales team. He had a great speaking voice, a strong work ethic, and truly cared about his current customers. But acquiring new customers was a different story—Lewis was the least successful salesperson of the group. Building rapport and gaining trust with strangers was difficult for him to achieve without a glimmer of a smile. Lewis's company's products and services helped other companies grow! This should be good news he was delivering, but his face told a very different story. *Not* smiling is this case was the real sign of weakness. Lewis needed to "face" the facts. Showing up in the world with a face of positive Calmfidence changes everything.

"Believe it or not, Lewis can have a pretty good sense of humor when he's not talking about work," the director of sales for the glass company whispered in my ear as she pulled me outside of the room before our next session was about to begin. This I had to see.

As the group entered the room for the afternoon session, I said, "Let's have a little fun to get the ball rolling again as we digest our lunch. We're going to forget about our presentations for a little while and take turns telling the group the funniest story that has ever happened to us or the funniest story we've ever heard. This is just a fun warm-up, no pressure, no presentation mode." Without anyone noticing, I rolled the camera. As each member of the sales team told their stories, I glanced in Lewis's direction and saw him smiling and chuckling to himself a few times. It was like looking at a different person.

When it was Lewis's turn to share his story, at first it was the same old expressionless Lewis. But as he got deeper into what became a hysterical story about him and his Marine buddies pranking each other, Lewis started smiling and laughing so hard that the entire room was in tears. Then we took a break.

After we regrouped, I played back some video. First I played a clip of Lewis's painful morning presentation. I immediately followed it with a clip of Lewis laughing and smiling, telling his story. The contrast was enormous. In the first clip Lewis looked hard and cold. In the second clip he looked likeable and approachable, the kind of person anyone would want to be around. I saw Lewis's jaw drop. I didn't say a word but just smiled at him. He gave me a hesitant smile and said: "I understand now. Boy, do I have a lot of work to do!"

Over the next few months, I had one-on-one sessions with Lewis, and he did put in the work. Smiling came easier for him after a while. New client sales increased rapidly over the next several months, culminating in Lewis receiving Salesperson of the Year at the company's annual awards dinner.

A Smile Is Worth a Thousand Connections

We've all heard the phrase "A smile is worth a thousand words." A smile is one of the most powerful nonverbal cross-cultural communication tools we have. A smile can speak louder than any words. Most important, a smile can create an instant connection with others. It communicates friendliness, openness, confidence, and positivity. A study published by the website Science Direct showed that genuine smiles induce trust and signal higher earning opportunities for people. The study also found that people who smile are perceived as more attractive and more intelligent than those who do not. People who do not smile can be perceived as untrustworthy, unfriendly, unprepared, nervous, or judgmental.

Let's Face It

Your entire face says a lot about you. Not just how you look, but how you feel, and even what you're thinking. It communicates a great deal to other people whether you want it to or not.

The human face has more than forty muscles, and they all can work independently of each other. The face can have a mind of its own and convey what we are feeling even when we don't want it to. It can send out unconscious messages—including some that we may not intend to communicate with others. Our faces can broadcast our moods, our health, how we feel about what is going on around us, and even our credibility.

Our face can also go flat. When people are afraid of public speaking, anxious about giving a presentation, or nervous about being interviewed, they get a deer-in-the-headlights look. Our faces go blank when we go blank. When we're processing information, feel like we're having an out-of-body experience, or just frozen from nerves, our face can become expressionless.

Your face has to tell the same story as your words. Otherwise people won't believe you and might not trust you. You can't convince them of what you're saying if they don't connect with how you are saying it. Genuine emotion is key. Your face is a canvas where emotion needs to live. Words without emotion are dead. We need to hear and see the whole package. Not only is it okay to be human, but also you *need* to be human when you are speaking in public, on stage, or in front of the camera.

When you choose not to smile or forget to make this human connection, you shut down one of the most important communication tools you have. This happens when we try to be perfect and flawless. It happens when we try too hard to be something that we think others want us to be. It happens when we *act*. The magic happens when we allow for our own humanity. Being real, human, and flawed is always better than being stone-faced, plastic, perfect, or hiding behind a mask, especially when it comes to public speaking or being a great communicator. When you are authentic, your facial communication is genuine, too.

From Sea to Shining "See"

It doesn't matter if you were born in a skyscraper in New York City or in a straw village on a remote island on the other side of the world; we all share facial expressions that convey common emotions. Psychologist Dr. Paul Ekman, a pioneer in the study of emotions, determined there are seven universal facial expressions that all humans share: fear, anger, sadness, happiness, disgust, contempt, and surprise. An extensive portion of the body language certification training I went through also focused on this.

Early naysayers disputed Ekman's findings, saying that these expressions could be a learned communication, as children learn to communicate by watching and imitating the faces of others as they develop. But psychologist Dr. David Matsumoto, a renowned expert in nonverbal behavior, studied the facial expressions of Paralympic athletes and found that no matter which country the athletes were from, they all had the same facial expression for each emotion. What really clinched his finding was that eight of those athletes were blind from birth.

MICRO-EXPRESSIONS

In addition to the seven universal facial expressions, there are micro-expressions, which happen in the blink of an eye. Micro-expressions are split-second leaks of true emotions that flash on the face before we hide them consciously. We often miss these when looking at others because they happen so fast. If you know what to look for, you can sometimes catch them. Micro-expressions will give you an unsettled feeling and a sense that something is not quite right. Think of emotions as a tree growing up from the ground: a person's intention would be the roots. Body language and facial expressions are the trunk. Thought and feelings are the branches, and words are the leaves.

When a person experiences an emotion, first there is intent or incident, then unconscious reaction or response (body language and facial expression), then conscious thought of the emotion, and finally expression with words. The body language and facial expression happen like a reflex at first. This is why there are a lot of bad actors out there. They're trying to express emotion through fake facial expressions or body language after they consciously express the emotion, when it should happen before. This can be true for liars as well. When the emotion is raw and real, in just a flash of a second, our face will leak a glimmer of that expression, even if we want to hide how we are feeling. This can happen when we're surprised by a piece of information that is unwelcome during a meeting or when we are uncomfortable in a social situation running into someone we weren't prepared to see.

If you could videotape every interaction you have with every person of both their face and yours and then view it frame by frame (about 28–30 frames per second), you could catch each micro-expression that either of you made during your conversation. Since you can't videotape your daily interactions, you can listen to your gut when trying to read another person.

When you get that uh-oh feeling that something isn't right or the impression that the other person didn't quite seem genuine, listen to your gut—because your subconscious may have caught a micro-expression. This should not lead you to jump to conclusions, but it should lead you to ask more questions, which in turn can open up a better line of communication. The flipside of this is that you leak these micro-expressions as well. So before any interaction, you need to get clear on how you feel about something and decide ahead of time what your intention is, what outcome you are aiming for, and how strongly you stand behind your true emotions, feelings, and beliefs.

Face Talk

What messages are you sending with your facial expressions? Are you giving the right impression, or are you giving the wrong impression? How good are you at reading the faces of your coworkers, loved ones, or strangers to know what they are thinking and feeling?

Here are some tips on how to read face talk:

- Real smiles need smiling eyes. Real smiles push up into your eyes and cause crow's feet at the outer corners of the eyes. When someone is faking a smile, the eyes won't be engaged like this.

- Not all smiles are positive. People also smile when they are embarrassed. People can smile in delight at other people's misfortune, also known as schadenfreude.

- When a person is experiencing real sadness, it shows in their eyebrows. The inner brows pull downward toward the bridge of the nose. The mouth will pout, quiver, or turn down at the corners. These facial movements do not occur when someone is faking sadness.

- When someone closes their eyes a lot, it could mean they are processing information, hiding something, or are uncomfortable.

- When we don't like what we hear, our lips disappear! The limbic system shuts down the mouth when a person can't take what they are hearing or experiencing. The jaw tightens and clenches.

- When a person puts their hand over their mouth or covers their lips with their hand or fingers, it may mean they are hiding something. Alternatively, they might be shocked or concerned over what they are hearing, or they may be afraid they might say the wrong thing.

- A wrinkled forehead could mean doubt, concern, anger, or confusion.

- When a person is angry, the eyebrows furrow, the jaw and teeth clench, the nose flares and the eyes get smaller.

- When a person is afraid, the eyes open and the mouth opens in a pulled-back manner tight into the jaw.

- When someone is feeling contempt, one side of their mouth goes up.

- When a person is disgusted, their face looks like they smell something bad, the sides of their lips go down, and their nose crinkles.

- When someone is surprised, their eyebrows rise, their eyes open wide, and their mouth forms an "o" shape.

- Be sure to look at the total picture: sum up what the eyebrows, mouth, eyes, chin, and jaw are doing in order to get a complete assessment of all nonverbal facial clues.

- To spot potential lies, look for micro-expressions but also look for hot spots—changes in facial expression that are different from someone's baseline or normal everyday facial expressions. If it's someone you just met during an interview or a meeting, notice his or her face during light and airy chat and see what changes take place during more intense or serious conversation. Be aware that your face will change too depending on how the interaction goes.

- When trying to read a person's face when they are wearing a mask, focus on the eyes. Look for crow's feet that indicate a genuine smile. Pay attention to eyebrows as well.

Mirror, Mirror

Have you ever considered that when you look in the mirror you are seeing the reverse or opposite image of how others see you? We are so used to seeing this mirror image of ourselves that this is one of the main reasons people don't like still photographs or videos of themselves: something looks different—and it is different—it's you in reverse! But do spend some time in the mirror really learning what your facial expressions look like. It might feel weird but it's another way to fully learn how to use your communication tools.

There is another type of mirror that we respond to as we interact with others. Mirroring is a behavior in which we match or mimic the emotions, facial expressions, and body language of the people we are communicating with. We tend to sync up all of these things when we are in rapport with each other. We can even line up our speech patterns, our attitude, and energy with those we feel a connection with. As we start to subconsciously mirror another person's facial expressions, a phenomenon called *emotional contagion* can happen where we catch the other person's emotional energy. So, your facial expressions can actually bring someone up to a positive state or bring him or her down to a negative place.

Facial Habits to Avoid

THE CHEEK CHEWER

I'll admit it. For years I've struggled with a bad habit of biting the inside of my mouth. When I flew to California for college spring break with five of my girlfriends, I was sitting next to an older woman on the plane who noticed me chewing away. She leaned over and said, "Honey, if you chew long enough you might get a big cancerous growth in there someday and lose your good looks." Yikes, you'd think that would have cured me of it, but it didn't quite. It's a subconscious bad habit that I still work on blocking today. Thankfully I never developed the cancerous growth, but chewing has contributed to some wrinkles around my mouth. I've been able to get a better handle on it since I went through my body language training.

Chewing the inside of your mouth sends the same message to others as biting your fingernails. It indicates that you might be nervous, stressed out, or unsure of yourself. I recently worked with a client who didn't even know she had the habit, too. I was helping her prepare for an important TV interview, and, after I played back the video of a mock interview we did, I pointed it out to her. She was shocked. She was also unhappy to see how it made her appear: nervous, unsure, even unprepared. She worked hard on eliminating the habit during the rest of our training session together.

Sometimes just knowing you have a bad habit like chewing, wrinkling your forehead or your nose, biting your lower lip, or licking your lips can help you work toward minimizing it. It's worth finding out what unknown bad habits you may have that could be sending the wrong message. Here are three things you can do to conquer the chew:

- Chew sugarless gum or keep a sugar-free hard candy or mint in your mouth. By giving yourself another option, you'll give your cheeks a break and disrupt the cycle a bit.

- Eat pineapple. The acidic nature of pineapple helps smooth out the tiny rough spots that make you want to chew more. It works fast!

- Ask friends and family to point out when they catch you chewing away at your cheek unconsciously. Mindfulness is a great step in putting the brakes on the mindless chew.

BITING LIPS SINK SHIPS

There was a slogan during World War II, "Loose Lips Sink Ships," put on posters to warn servicemen and citizens to be careful not to talk about any information that could possibly benefit the enemy. After the war, this phrase became a common expression that people would use to tell others to avoid careless talk that could affect business, a new product launch, ruin the surprise party, let the cat out of the bag—you get where I'm going. In a similar way when it comes to communication skills, biting your lips can sink your ship. When people are nervous, uncomfortable, unsure, unprepared, or up to something, they tend to bite or nibble on their lower lip. This is a *tell* in body language that sends a red flag. When job interviewers see it, they take notice. When it's done during a speech or a TV appearance it speaks volumes. Licking lips also sends the same type of message. Many times, when my clients get nervous they get dry mouth and their lips get dry too. They play with their lip with their teeth or tongue to get back moisture or because a dry piece of lip keeps poking at them. They may not be nervous at all, but sadly they are sending the wrong message because their lips are annoying them. Women can counteract this with lipstick and lip gloss to add moisture and are less likely to bite or lick so they don't mess up their makeup or eat their lipstick. Men can help prevent licking and biting their lip by making sure to apply a clear lip balm, especially before a big speech, interview, or meeting. Keep it on hand to reapply as needed.

DISTRACTING FACIAL EXPRESSIONS

You'd be amazed at how many distracting facial habits come out when I'm videotaping my clients during media and public-speaking training sessions. The good news is that once I point out distracting habits and they see them for themselves on the screen, they work to break bad habits and can do so pretty quickly. This is another good reason to practice speaking or interviewing while you videotape yourself. There's a wealth of information you can uncover about yourself. Here are a few of my favorite facial expressions that I love to hate:

- The Groucho Marx: when people raise their eyebrows excessively, and especially when there's no reason to do it, when it does not match their words or intentions.

- The Grimace: when people look like they have a stomachache, they're overly concerned, or they've just witnessed someone swallow a watermelon whole.

- The Excessive Blinker: be sure to take care of any dry-eye issues ahead of time, clean your contact lenses, relax your eyes, and slow down.

- The Nose Toucher: the human nose contains erectile tissue that can become slightly swollen or engorged with blood when someone is telling a lie, agitated, or nervous. This can cause an itch or tingle that makes someone touch or scratch their nose. The nose touch is considered a body language *tell* that might mean something's up. You could simply have a cold or allergy, but when you touch your nose during a speech, meeting, or interview, it might make others think differently.

- Resting bitch face (RBF): this is when someone's neutral or *expressionless* face is not exactly neutral. Some people don't realize that when they are intensely listening to someone, processing information, or trying to look cool, they may think they're not showing any expression but their face is off-putting to others. They may look slightly annoyed, bored, or judgmental. Studies have shown that in the case of RBF, the face gives an impression of contempt, disrespect, disgust, or arrogance. A look of contempt can be very subtle, with one side of the mouth slightly tilting up and sometimes with the eyes squinting a bit. It can be a flash, like a micro-expression, or a deliberate expression to tell someone exactly what you think. But if your resting face has this look, oh boy, just think of the messages you are sending to others around you.

I've had plenty of clients who work in front of the camera, or in sales, or with the public in some way who had no idea they had RBF until it revealed itself during a training session. I wonder how many people they turned off before they knew what their face was doing (and saying). I was recently sitting in on a training session being taught by another coach. As I looked around the room, I noticed one guy staring at the trainer as she reviewed a PowerPoint with the class. I didn't know this guy at all, but I immediately felt annoyed by him. I caught myself and wondered what was it about him that made me feel this way. I hadn't even heard him speak yet. Then I saw it. The left side of his lips curled up just a bit, in a slight look of contempt, as if he wasn't buying what the trainer was selling. I looked back at the trainer to see if she was picking up on it. Then he asked a question, and he was obviously a nice guy who was there to learn—he likely had no idea his face was sending the wrong message. If he was a client of mine, I would suggest that he try to consciously balance his *listening face* by slightly raising the right side of his lips so that his expression would show at the very least that he is happy to be there (wherever there is!). In television there is a term called *active listening*. Active listening is what producers and directors love to see on the faces of people who are not the ones doing the talking at the moment. Because television is all about the visual, we can tell just by a person's face if they are fully engaged and in the moment with what is going on around them or not. A great cohost, interviewer, or interviewee will have appropriate facial emotions and expressive personality when it's their turn to simply listen. RBF makes for terrible television and in-person interactions, unless your intention really is to show contempt, dissatisfaction, annoyance, or disgust.

Facial Credibility

Let's talk a bit about makeup. Makeup isn't just about beauty and glamour; for both men and women, it can be an important tool to look calm, cool, and collected. But many people who do not like to wear makeup resist the idea that there may be times when it is necessary.

A few years ago I was hired to do a media training presentation for the American Medical Association's Health Communicators Conference in Florida. At the reception I was speaking with a woman surgeon who was adamant about never wearing makeup and not seeing the need to change this just because she was going to be interviewed on television. She felt it was a credibility issue. It was extremely important to her to not appear as if she was concerned about her appearance and the need to make herself up with things like lipstick and blush. While I totally respected and understood her position on this, I asked her to also consider a different perspective. Television is often a place where people try to look and act natural in a very unnatural setting. A studio is flooded with lights. Camera angles, unnatural lighting, shadows, set colors, wardrobe, and background colors can all wash out and overwhelm everyday makeup, let alone no makeup. The same goes for stage lighting when giving a presentation, or public speaking at an event. In addition, both men and women sweat under these circumstances. This can make people appear washed-out, tired, shiny, and as if they just don't have their act together.

It's always a good idea to consult with a professional makeup artist who is on-set or at the event, or with a top-notch makeup retailer for advice on appropriate makeup for television, stage, or events. Even a great colorless absorbing powder can sometimes do wonders to give the appearance of cool Calmfidence.

Facial Calmfidence increases your Calm communication skills by:

- Knowing how to communicate quietly without having to say a word.
- Trusting the messages your face is revealing to the world.
- Using smiles to break down barriers and help others feel comfortable.

Facial Calmfidence increases your confident communication skills by:

- Knowing how to build rapport nonverbally.
- Being more aware of how to use our nonverbal facial expressions to be perceived more positively by others.
- Understanding how to best present yourself to increase your credibility.

Being in tune with your facial Calmfidence makes you a better communicator because you know and trust the nonverbal messages you are sending with your facial expressions and habits. Understanding the facial expressions and habits of others helps you to notice and identify what they may be thinking and feeling in addition to what they are actually saying to you. And this brings us to our next chapter on nonverbal communication skills: "Body-Language Calmfidence."

Calmfidence Reflections

List any bad facial habits you think you might have and would like to change:

_____

_____

_____

List three ways you can utilize your smile more to make yourself and others feel more comfortable:

_____

_____

_____

List a few ways you can be a better facial communicator:

_____

_____

_____

13

Body-Language Calmfidence

People may not tell you how they feel about you,
but they always show you. Pay attention.

Keri Hilson

In addition to my work coaching and training, I frequently work as a health and wellness medical anchor, traveling the country with a digital broadcast company to interview medical professionals. "I'd like to introduce you all to Doctor Ashley, our guest medical expert for today's live satellite broadcast," our executive producer said as he escorted the polished forty-something brunette into our studio. Her perfectly tailored steel-gray designer suit was only outdone by her black patent-leather Christian Louboutin high-heel pumps with their fire-engine-red soles. "Hello," she said in the general direction of the room, without making eye contact with anyone. Her energy was as cold and gray as her suit.

"Doctor Ashley, please sit next to Patricia, our host and moderator. She'll be interviewing you on the show today," the producer said. As my guest took her place in the seat next to me, her bedside manner did not improve. I'm accustomed to working with physicians with different personalities, some friendly and easy-going, some more aloof and reserved. Today it seemed I was going to have to deal with the latter. All I could think was, *This is going to be a long show.*

As we read through the script and rehearsed the show, I noticed something rapidly flashing under the table that no one else could see. Doctor Ashley's shiny red-bottomed heels were bouncing a mile a minute. From the waist up she was working overtime to appear cool and collected, but her feet betrayed her. She was a nervous wreck. Her attempt to fake calm and confidence had prevented her from feeling comfortable with me and the team, and everyone assumed she was an ice queen. Luckily for her, I now knew what to do to help her have a great show.

"Doctor Ashley, let's get a cup of coffee and chat a bit more about our interview," I said, after we were done doing the rundown on the set. I wanted a few minutes alone with her. As we walked down the hallway to the kitchen area, I made a bit of small talk about her family and where she'd flown in from that day.

"Have you ever been on TV before, Doctor?" I asked.

"No, I haven't. This is my first television interview," she replied.

"It's my job to make you look and sound fantastic today, Doctor Ashley. My goal is to make you feel as comfortable as possible and fully support you. So please let me know how I can help," I said.

Her demeanor completely changed, and she gave a deep sigh of relief. "I didn't want anyone to know it, but I was extremely nervous walking in here today. I'm sorry if I came off a bit cold with my poker face. You've made me feel so much better just knowing that you are here to help me have a successful interview. Thank you for pulling me aside."

Everything changed after that conversation. The show was great. The interview was engaging and informative. If I hadn't tuned in to those bouncing feet below the table, I would have never known that the doctor was so nervous and been able to help her.

Your Nonverbal Communication Skills

Body-language Calmfidence is being aware of the nonverbal signals you are sending out, as well as being able to notice and identify the signals that other people are giving off.

Over the years I've studied many body-language books and research articles. I've worked with thousands of clients and students to help them overcome body-language problems, which they often didn't even know they had. I showed them how to be more comfortable, open, and expressive and to exude Calmfidence. Because I wanted even more research and knowledge to add to my training programs, I attended a body-language trainer certification program in Washington, DC.

During each day of our training, we viewed frame-by-frame video analysis of serial killers, embezzlers, athletes accused of doping and cheating, crooked politicians, sex offenders, murderers, and garden-variety liars. We had intense homework assignments each night. I figured if I could learn to diagnose these extreme examples of body language, facial expression, and verbal statements, I could bring valuable information to my clients. And I learned a tremendous amount about reading nonverbal messages that we send and observe. The most important takeaway from my training, however, was the understanding that reading body language is not the same as reading minds. Interpreting people's body language should lead you to ask better questions about the person and the situation, but it should not lead you to make assumptions.

Here's some of what I've learned over the past twenty years of communication training and research, combined with the knowledge from training in reading body language.

Own Your Space

How we live in our own space speaks volumes. Whether you are sitting or standing, are you making yourself larger or smaller? If you want to show Calmfidence, you have to open up and claim the space around you. Your presence tells people how you feel about yourself and how they should feel about you. It also tells YOU how you feel about yourself! Changing your body language can change your attitude, your emotional state, and even your hormone levels.

TAKE A STAND

Stand tall, chin up, shoulders back, weight evenly distributed between your feet, feet firmly on the ground separated eight to ten inches apart. Assume the kind of stance where you wouldn't get knocked down if someone bumped into you. Notice how you stand when you are waiting in line for a coffee or your lunch. Are your hands relaxed down by your sides, or are you slouching, covering, blocking, crossing, minimizing, shoving your hands in your pockets, or fidgeting? When we're used to standing a certain way, opening up can feel awkward, vulnerable, and even naked. But the more you practice it, the more Calmfidence you will have.

My father in-law was a police officer in the Bronx Task Force, and he told me that this is how police officers are trained to approach people—hands down by their sides, not hidden in their pockets or behind their backs, open, sure-footed, and showing Calmfidence.

In my late teens I worked at a women's clothing store in the local mall. My manager always commented on a particular female customer who would come to shop for business suits. She pointed out what a great presence the woman had, how she carried herself with confidence yet was still approachable. She stood tall and commanded the air and space around her, not in an arrogant way, but in a way that said, "I know who I am and I like myself." She owned her body, owned her space, and was incredibly friendly. She was the spark in the room. I began to copy the way she carried herself. In that clothing store I was trying something else on for size: Calmfidence. The more I mimicked her body language, the more Calmfidence I started to feel.

Many women sell themselves short with their body language. Nothing will minimize your presence more than bad posture. Oftentimes we are subconsciously making ourselves smaller and giving away our power when we fold into ourselves with rolled shoulders, chins down. Women of all heights do this when they don't want to draw attention to themselves. But for tall women this can be especially true. Many tall women who are great at building rapport and getting on the same level with other people around them consciously or subconsciously attempt to make others comfortable by hunching over so they aren't towering over those around them. Believe me, if you're tall everyone knows it and you should celebrate it. I'd love another five or six inches of height myself!

Poor posture is considered the number-one body language sign of uncertainty, lack of confidence, low energy, discouragement, and submissiveness. When your parents told you to stand up straight and keep your chin up, they had very good reason.

Studies show that tall people may interrupt short people more often or try to intimidate them. This can be especially true for women who are shorter than their male counterparts. Maximize your presence by leveling the playing field. Find ways to stand while others sit during meetings, negotiations, or pitches. If you're about to have a personal or confrontational conversation, be sure to sit down with that taller friend or family member so that you can speak at the same level, eye to eye. I've heard people refer to petite people who have great posture and a dynamic presence as having a "tall" personality!

A WALLFLOWER HAS NO POWER

Recently I was training a female CEO of a large pharmaceutical company in presentation and public-speaking skills. When she stood up to rehearse her presentation, she stood small, feet close together, shoulders rounded forward and down, hands clasped modestly in front of her pelvis. She looked more like a wallflower or someone attending a funeral than a powerful, smart female CEO. Her body was telling us a very different story from her job title and résumé.

When I pointed this out to her, she told me that she recently was at an event where she watched a group of presenters on a stage and noticed how the two women in the group stood this same way, and she thought they looked "nice and demure." Really? How is that a good thing? I quickly called up the definition of *demure* on my phone and read it to her: "reserved, modest, and shy." I continued to read the example used in a sentence: "a demure little wife who sits at home minding the house." She had mentioned that none of the men on stage stood this way. They stood tall and open to the audience. We corrected her stance, and the results were astounding. She instantly looked and felt stronger and more dynamic. Today when you are out and about in your daily life, pay attention to how you live in your space and how you hold yourself when you are standing or waiting in line. When I have my clients do this in their personal lives it really makes a difference for them the next time they present in front of a room or in front of the camera.

POSITIVE POSTURE

Think about how you feel when you are having a bad day and you just lie around in your PJs or sweatpants all day. Do you think you'd be up for a phone interview for a job or that confrontational call you've been dreading? Probably not, since you've been in a retreat mode both in your body and mind. Now think about how you feel when you are having a great day, feeling comfortable in your own skin, enthusiastic and hopeful. Your posture is strong, there's a skip in your step, and your head is high. Either one of these days would have a ripple effect on how you think about yourself and how you interact with the people around you.

YOUR SHARE OF THE CHAIR

When people with Calmfidence sit in chairs, you can barely even see the chair. They've got their arms hanging over the sides of the chair, they're using them as stretching devices, relaxation seats, pondering perches, and hangout hammocks. Being comfortable in your own skin makes every chair more comfortable to sit in. Of course, you have to judge each situation accordingly: you shouldn't sprawl in your chair in exaggerated positions in professional settings, but you can be open and comfortable to different degrees when you read the room and people around you. Don't just sit in your chair. Use your chair to feel powerful, accessible, comfortable, and fully present. This could be as simple as resting your arm over the chairback rather than sitting with your hands neatly placed in your lap or on the desk or table in front of you. Again, maximize your space, don't minimize it.

WALKIE-TALKIE

My grandfather always told me to walk like you are on a mission—like you are on your way to do great things. I once worked with an emcee who told me that before he walked onto any stage, he would pretend that he had just come from someplace amazing. The way we hold ourselves when we walk sends powerful energy out all around us, and people can feel it. I love watching people walk through New York City. Some look like they are wandering, some look like they are lost, some look overwhelmed, and some look like they are just going through their daily grind. Then there are those people who look like they are on a mission—like they've got some place to go. They walk with determination, purpose, and passion. It's palpable. You can feel their energy. They are shining. How wonderful to walk through life this way. The next time you get on your way, walk with purpose; you will arrive with a different mindset. People will generally get out of the way of a person who looks like they are moving in their direction with determination. Don't we all feel good, safe, and assured when we are around people who know where they are going? Here are some surefire ways that you can walk with purpose and radiate Calmfidence in your steps:

- Walk with big steps like you have someplace to go.
- A wide stride gives the impression you are *getting the job done.*
- Walk with awareness of what's going on all around you.
- Walk into rooms like you are glad to be there and interested to see and meet all those who are there.
- Your posture is the very first thing that people notice about your body. Walk and stand tall.

You Soothe, You Lose

Self-touch can be soothing, but usually *when we are soothing, we are losing.* When we're stressed, unsure of ourselves, uncomfortable, or feeling vulnerable, we unconsciously look for ways to feel better. Touch is very reassuring. If there's no one there to reach out and touch us, we do it ourselves. Self-touch is a pacifier. Just like a baby sucks its thumb or a pacifier, touch is a natural reaction, an instant fix to feel good, to pacify oneself. Sometimes, doing something that makes you feel better is okay, but it all depends on the situation. If you're in a job interview or a professional setting where people are looking to rely on someone who they can trust to get the job done, you don't want to be sending messages that indicate that you need reassurance. If you're dealing with any kind of stressful situation and you don't want your anxiety to show, watch out for these self-touch, self-soothing giveaways:

- Rubbing hands together
- Rubbing wrist, forearm, or shoulder
- Rubbing back of neck

- Spinning in chair
- Picking at fingernails or cuticles
- Playing with jewelry
- Playing with hair
- Covering mouth with hand or fingers
- Biting nails
- Biting a pen or pencil
- Biting eyeglass stems
- Pacing
- Fidgeting
- Fixing hair
- Adjusting clothing

A client who is a host on a popular cable TV channel had a habit of twisting his wedding ring when he read the news on camera. He said it was a ritual for him—something that he felt was a "signature" of his. He didn't realize that although this was what it meant to him, it gave a very different impression to the viewers. The ring twisting prevented him from using his natural gestures, blocked his energy flow, and made him less open to the camera. It also made viewers look at his hands and take their focus off his face and the information he gave. Worst of all, it gave the impression that he was nervous, as most self-soothing habits do. Not a good look for TV and not good for his credibility.

Get a Head Start

You can say a lot with the way you tilt your head. The old saying that someone has their "head on straight" means that they've got it together, they're sure of themselves, or they have a handle on the situation. It is said that when people tilt their head to the left they are perceived as being more intelligent and when they tilt their head to the right they appear more attractive. So, depending on your goals, think about what would be more beneficial in the situation you are in. Men tend to hold their heads up straight when they are negotiating, in a conversation, or listening to someone. Women tend to tilt their heads to one side or the other, which can sometimes look submissive. I believe that the strongest head position for negotiation, determination, or a Calmfidence presence is straight up and down. However, if you are trying to show compassion and empathy, then a head tilt can send a warmer, more understanding and caring message.

THE "GET ME OUT OF HERE" VEER

The first time I get people to do a training exercise in front of the camera, I commonly see the head veer. This is when the head slightly turns and veers to the left or the right and a person looks like they are talking out of the side of their mouth. Or they tilt their head back, away from the camera, and lead with their chin as they speak. What I see when someone does this is that they want to get away. They want to get this over with as fast as possible and to get through this so they can be *done*. Side talking looks incredibly uncomfortable in front of the camera or in person. It's unappealing and makes it hard for the viewer to connect with you. When someone tilts their head back and leads with their chin, it ends up looking like they are talking down their nose to people, which can come across as arrogant. No one really wants to look up someone's nostrils anyway, especially if they have a cold.

During a media-training session with an international TV host, I noticed he kept pulling rigidly to one side. I asked him if he was uncomfortable being in front of the camera. He wasn't, but he had been told by some well-meaning public relations advisor that one side of his face was his "better side." So he constantly favored turning his perceived good side toward the camera, which made him look stiff and odd even though he was extremely attractive. I couldn't imagine that anyone would think he had a bad side. We worked for quite some time to undo this advice so that he could relax and use his head in a more natural way when in front of the camera.

Your best "side" is actually facing forward with your face aimed directly at whomever you're addressing. The most important person you're talking with is the one who is right in front of you, either in person or through the lens.

THE CHIN IS IN

You tell people a lot with just your chin. A level chin looks direct and in charge. A chin tilted just slightly down can look alluring and attractive.

A person whose chin dips down very low seems as if they are trying to minimize their presence or hide. You'll see someone's chin ultra-low when they are depressed, disinterested, embarrassed, or afraid.

The way we touch our chin with our hands can tell the world very different things. If we are resting the weight of our chin or jawline on our hand, we can look bored or tired, but if we are resting our hand or finger on our chin, we appear intelligent and contemplative, as if considering our options or assessing a situation or person. My body language instructors would say: "When you grab your chin you're about to win!"

DON'T BE A BOBBLE HEAD

We help other people communicate by the way we listen to their stories. Our eyes, eyebrows, lips, and head nods let them know we are hearing them, understanding them, or are interested in what they are saying. The speed and number of nods tells the other person a lot about how we feel. A couple of slow nods say that we are listening, we are with them. Lots of fast head nods say "Hurry up, move on, yeah, I already know that," and the like. In interviewing many guests on television shows, I learned that my head nods could help a nervous guest get through an interview smoothly or hurry them up if they were long-winded and needed to wrap it up.

When I coach people for television interviews and job interviews, I warn them to beware of the agreement nod. Many times, we unconsciously nod to communicate that we understand someone's question, but don't realize it could come across that we agree with what they are saying when we may not, even before we have a chance to answer their question.

The Hands Have It

GIVE A THUMBS UP

Hitch a ride on the Calmfidence bus and give yourself the *thumbs up*. When people are nervous or stressed, their thumbs tend to disappear, either into their pockets or tucked into their fists. When we hide our thumbs, we tell the world that we need to be reassured. To look confident, keep your hands out of your pockets and keep your thumbs visible. The only exception to this rule is the thumb hook, that cool-dude move when you hook your thumb on one or both of your jeans pockets with most of your thumb still visible and the rest of your hand outside.

STEEPLE CHASE

One of the most powerful body-language gestures is called the steeple. The steeple is when you place your hands together, palms facing, fingers spread apart and touching each matching finger at the tips. It looks like a steeple on a church. It's the favorite of CEOs, deep thinkers, high-power celebrities, and strategic negotiators. It exemplifies intelligence, thoughtfulness, Calmfidence, and composure, but it can be used in the wrong place and at the wrong time. It wouldn't be a great gesture trying to build rapport at a PTA meeting, on the playground or a first date, or when meeting your spouse's family for the first time. It can be seen as arrogant when used in a setting that calls for warmth and casual conversation. The basketball steeple is a similar gesture only expanded to look as though you could literally be holding an invisible basketball. This gesture works well when you are giving a speech and sharing a vision, presenting an idea about which you're passionate, or explaining a concept that you want your audience to imagine and accept or adopt.

A NICE GESTURE

We need to use our hands to communicate. Gestures actually help us speak. Like the motions of a conductor in front of an orchestra, our hands and arms help us tell a story. They show our intensity and passion. Gestures help us describe the size and distance of things, and they can even replace words and phrases. When people don't speak with their hands, they can seem uptight, stiff, expressionless, and lackluster.

Just like we don't like a monotone voice or monotone facial expression, we don't like monotone body language either. Remember, we need voice, face, and body to congruently be telling the same story, or something just doesn't seem right. Beware the "monotone zone"!

HAND TO THROAT

Our neck dimple, which is the hollow of the neck just below the Adam's apple and above the top of the breast bone, is a place that we cover and protect when we hear something that shocks us, frightens us, or threatens us. Often, we do it as we are saying, "Oh, my God!" or "Oh, no!" If you subconsciously cover your neck dimple with your hand during a negotiation, interview, or confrontational conversation, however, you could be sending the message that you are shocked, intimidated, or threated by what you are hearing. This would be bad if you didn't want the other person to know exactly how you were feeling about the situation. Keep your hands away from your throat when you don't want to let that salesman know you think the price is too high, or let your boss know that you are intimidated by that latest assignment.

THE FIG LEAF IS A THIEF

One of the most popular places to cover ourselves with clasped hands is over our private area, or what some body-language experts refer to as *naughty bits*. This gesture has been dubbed "the fig-leaf pose" in just about every book on body language and public speaking. We subconsciously protect this area when we are stressed, concerned, or worried. When you cover or block this area with your hands, you are going into protective mode and will no longer appear to be standing or sitting in an open, accessible, or strong position.

PALMING THIGHS

When we are stressed and the palms of our hands get sweaty, we tend to subconsciously wipe them against our thighs in an attempt to dry them. Palming thighs is almost always indicative of pacifying oneself, an attempt to get rid of nervous energy, or a dead giveaway that we are wiping off sweat to try to hide our stress.

Foot Loose

When someone's feet are pointed away from another person during a conversation, it shows that they want to get out of there. Their body is expressing that they want or need to leave, they are already half out the door, or they are interested in other things or other people in the room where their feet are pointing.

When we are stressed or nervous, we tend to bounce our feet and legs while seated and shuffle them on the floor when we are standing. I've even witnessed people wrapping their ankles around the bottom of a chair when they are feeling stressed out. When we are truly engaged in a conversation with someone, everything is pointing in their direction—feet, belly buttons, and chins—and we are still.

Don't Shrug It Off!

Remember that identifying one body-language sign does not make you a mind reader. Think of body-language signals as "hot spots" that should be investigated along with the bigger picture and measured against a person's baseline, their normal relaxed behavior. When you see a hot spot, it should lead you to ask questions about how the person is feeling. One stand-alone body-language sign may not end up meaning anything. But when someone shrugs their shoulders, it always means something: indecision, uncertainty, or disinterest. Pay attention to someone's shoulder shrugs when you are in a conversation. In turn, keep a check on when you are shrugging your own shoulders. Know that when you shrug you are sending a very definite message that you are not so definite!

GESTURES THAT CAN LOSE TRUST OR HURT RAPPORT

There are many gestures that can prevent bonding and make it harder to build a connection with those around us.

Leaning Away

Generally when people are engaged and interested, they lean toward people and ideas they like. Leaning away sends the opposite message. Picture a classroom or audience. Attendees who are enthusiastic or eager to learn are more forward-leaning toward the speaker in the front of the room. Those disinterested or unimpressed may veer back or slouch into their seats. This can be true in an interview situation or during a sales pitch as well.

Crossing Arms

When someone crosses their arms it can be a sign that the person is blocking themselves off from others. I really dislike when professionals choose to stand with crossed arms in promotional photos or headshots for this reason. It can be perceived as unapproachable. A caveat here is that it could possibly mean they are simply cold, or they are firmly staying put because they ARE interested in what they are hearing. Again, reading body language should help you to ask better questions to avoid making assumptions.

Hiding Arms Behind Back

Also known as the parade stance, hiding arms clasped behind one's back can make those around you feel uncomfortable. It might look like you are hiding something. It also prevents you from using your gestures in an open and expressive manner. It can come across as stiff and awkward—as if the person is a statue without arms. Keeping arms relaxed and hands visible is always a better choice.

Hands in Pockets

When communicating with others, placing hands in one's pockets also prevents relaxed open gestures from happening naturally. I've seen clients do this during presentations, and they end up jiggling loose change or keys in their pocket as they try to release nervous energy. Often when people feel stressed, they quickly shove their hands inside their pockets as well. People will sometimes choose to stand this way in an attempt to look relaxed and casual, but it's best to keep hands available for expression and openness.

A Calmfidence Cue Will Come True

Your body can literally set the tone and foundation for your day, an event, an interview, or any interpersonal interaction. When you give your body Calmfidence cues, soon they'll come true. If you are not feeling your best, most powerful self, you can change that by changing the way you use your body. You have the power to create biochemical reactions in your body that give you more Calmfidence. Do the body language first: *build it and they will come!*

Before an interview, speech, tough conversation, or negotiation, or anytime you have to stand up for yourself, physically stand up for yourself! Stand up straight, hold up your head, open up your body language, stand sturdy on your feet, avoid self-touch, uncross your arms and legs, and let your body tell the story that you are ready for whatever comes your way. The first few times you do this, you might feel exposed, awkward, or strange, but the more you condition yourself to stand (and sit) in powerful and open ways, the sooner you will actually become more powerful and have more Calmfidence.

Now that you know how to present yourself with calm and confidence using your body language, let's bring these empowering skills into the spotlight as we move on to "Public-Speaking Calmfidence."

Body-language Calmfidence increases your calm communication skills by:

- Knowing how to present calm gestures and avoid habits that express stress.

- Having self-awareness of how to set a calm tone for others around you with your body language for an event, an interview, or any interpersonal interaction.

- Changing your body language to affect your attitude, emotional state, and stress level.

Body-language Calmfidence increases your confident communication skills by:

- Being aware of the nonverbal messages your body is communicating.

- Acknowledging that when we're used to minimizing our presence, opening up and claiming our space can feel awkward, vulnerable, and scary. But the more you practice it, the more Calmfidence you will have.

- Knowing how to have a powerful presence using open body language, posture, gestures, and positioning.

- Knowing how to interpret the body-language signs of those around you so that you can ask more powerful questions to gain a better understanding of their emotions and needs.

Calmfidence Reflections

List three ways you may be minimizing your presence with your body language:

_____

_____

_____

List three ways you could use your body language to maximize your presence and appear more confident:

_____

_____

_____

List three ways you can use your body language to appear calmer:

_____

_____

_____

What are three things you will now look for when observing another person's body language?

_____

_____

_____

14

Public-Speaking
Calmfidence

All speaking is public speaking
whether it's to one person or a thousand.

Roger Love

I didn't have to give my first big presentation in front of a classroom until I was in a college business class. My thin, pale, serious teacher chewed the inside of her cheek, but she was tough. My assignment was to talk about the stock market, and I was nervous. My father suggested that I bring in an interesting fact about the origin of the terms *bulls* and *bears* that business reporters use when talking about the financial markets.

I learned that when bulls fight, they push up with their horns, and when bears fight, they swat down with their paws. Thus, a bull market is up, and a bear market is down. I was pleased with the material I had put together for my speech but sat in class dreading when my name would be called. When it was my turn, the walk through the classroom seemed very long and I thanked God that I would speak behind a podium, because it would block my trembling legs. But I learned a very important lesson that day. After I was done, and I survived, my professor came up to me to tell me that she had never heard my tidbit of bull/bear trivia before and that she was tickled and impressed to learn it from my speech. I was so relieved. And I couldn't believe that this cold woman was actually giddy. That was my first wow moment. I learned that my nerves didn't matter to people if I gave them something of value.

Most of us at some point have to speak in front of a room of people. It may be to a small group of people we know or a large room filled with strangers. The majority of people, not just you, aren't comfortable in either situation. After all, it's not something most people do every day, which is why it's so uncomfortable to do. If it was something you had to do all the time, you would eventually get used to it and get better at it. So, what do you do if you're not used to it and think you're not good at it? Let's break it down.

Why You?

First, think about why you're giving the presentation in the first place. Does someone else think you'll do a good job? Is it part of your job? Is it a message that's important to you personally? Look at the flipside of that—why is it important to your audience that you are speaking to them? The first thing most people think to themselves is, "What if I screw up?" "What if I sound silly?" "What if I lose my place or my heart pounds and my mouth gets dry?" We focus on the wrong things. We focus on ourselves. *What if, what if, what if,* and *I, I, I.* Yes, you are the messenger, the expert of the moment, the teacher, the presenter, the one in the front of the room, at the microphone, in the spotlight—but it really isn't about you at all.

It's Not About You

This is the key: it's not about you. It's has to be about your audience. How can you help them understand something? How can you educate them, encourage them, empower them, or entertain them? What do they want and need to get out of this presentation? Give them something of value. Make the audience your priority. It's the all-about-THEM show. Get out of your head and out of your own way. Take the focus off of yourself and focus on being of service to your audience. One of the biggest culprits of debilitating stage fright is being hyper-focused on ourselves.

Embrace Nervous Energy

Being nervous is a good thing. So often, people get nervous about being nervous! If you walk into a presentation or interview without any nervous energy, you will come across like a dud. Just because you're nervous doesn't mean you aren't going to do a good job. We need that nervous energy to get our juices flowing.

As a very young reporter at my first small TV station in New York, I had the great fortune to interview the legendary actor of stage and screen Helen Hayes. My station's team was playing in a local celebrity charity softball game against prominent people from our county. I was very green and nervous but thrilled to sit down in the dugout right next to Ms. Hayes with my list of questions. She was warm and friendly and very open. I apologized for being so nervous.

She looked at me and said, "Honey, when I stop getting nervous, put me in my coffin! That'll mean I'm done!"

I was confused. How could this famous and talented actor, who had then been in the spotlight for more than half a century, still get nervous? I asked her to explain.

She told me, "Butterflies in the stomach are a good thing. They make you sharp. They show that you still have passion and desire. They mean that you care." She went on to tell me that her biggest fear was losing that fire in her belly and becoming complacent. Nervous energy is filled with excitement, vibrancy, courage, and daring. She never wanted to lose that thrill that made her feel alive. She told me to welcome those butterflies but to also remember that it's our job to make them "fly in formation and work for us, not against us."

She suggested I change the label of *nervous* energy to *excited* energy—excitement for the opportunity. Without those nerves, we can come across as unenthusiastic or just going through the motions. I'd rather sit in the audience and listen to a presenter who has some nervous energy than one who is flat, unaffected, dispassionate, and just trying to get this over with. And again, just because you are nervous, that doesn't mean you won't do a good job. Lots of people do great things when they do things in spite of their nerves.

Let Go of Any Negative Past Experiences

Never hang around with your failures. Never talk about them. Never think about them. Leave bad public speaking experiences behind you. Don't let past performances define you as a speaker. Often, we carry around our failures like a heavy set of weights dragging behind us, slowing us down, tiring us out. We cannot change the past; what's done is done. Why relive it in your mind over and over again? Let it go. Move on. Keep moving forward. There are several ways you can do this. I used to write down things that I thought I had failed at on a piece of paper, crumple up that paper, and throw it into the garbage. Somehow the physical act of discarding that piece of the past made it easier to put it behind me and be done with it. Another way is to type your experience into a document and then delete it on your computer as you picture deleting it from your mind. Yes, we can and should learn from our mistakes, but if we keep replaying them, they will become roadblocks instead of pathways. Don't let that one bad speech haunt you. Don't let a bad experience or outcome lower your expectations of future attempts. Let each day and each new experience be a clean slate.

The Dreaded Launch

So many of my clients speak about those first few excruciating moments just prior to a presentation. They dread this time because of their body's reactions: a racing heart and mind. But once they get past those first few moments, they begin to feel level as their body adjusts. I was discussing this with a potential client over the phone when I was suddenly struck with the analogy of a rocket launch. Think of all the pressure, burning hot fuel, smoke, and effort that are needed for a rocket to lift off from the launching pad. Once it breaks out of the atmosphere and enters space, it floats calmly and the pressure is gone.

For public speaking, if we don't do it often, we dread it, fight it, and tell ourselves we shouldn't be feeling all this pressure, energy, or physical and emotional reactions. Why do we think this? It's part of the territory. Let's allow ourselves to be okay with feeling uncomfortable. It's an important part of a successful launch into a journey that we are taking with our audience. Let's give ourselves permission to trust ourselves as the captains of the ship when we are in front of the room, about to take the audience on an incredible ride, knowing that these feelings are part of the thrill of it all.

But how do we get to that point? First, realize that adrenaline makes you sharp and gives you the ability to be powerful and dynamic in front of a group of other human beings. Second, keep in mind that no matter how nervous you are, generally once you get past the first twenty seconds you will level out and feel better. So, commit to being courageous for just twenty seconds—most anyone can do that.

Third, start to label these nervous feelings differently. Associate them with the idea that something exciting is about to happen. You have the opportunity to help others in some way. Ask any seasoned speaker and they'll tell you that once they started getting desensitized to those excited butterflies, they needed to look for ways to get themselves energized before a speech so they wouldn't come across lackluster. It's the same reason that some athletes and adventurers up the ante and turn to more extreme sports over time. They get used to the rush and need to find a new one.

Put Your Cape On

That rush is part of the territory when it comes to speaking in front of others. It actually prepares your body and mind to handle the task in front of you if you understand and embrace its power. Adrenaline is our hormonal superpower. It's nitro for our engine, heightening and maximizing all our senses. We've all heard the story of a mother who is suddenly able to lift up a car to pull her baby out of harm's way. We've heard of heroic acts of saving others from danger that seem superhuman. That's adrenaline. That's the same liquid gold that's running through your veins when you get that fight-or-flight feeling. If adrenaline has enabled a person to lift a three-thousand-pound car, that same power can be harnessed and used by you, not against you, to give you Calmfidence. When you feel that adrenaline kick in, do not think *Oh, no! I'm nervous, and nervous is bad!* Rather, tell yourself *Here comes my super-fuel! I can go the distance and take on the world!*

Let's go back to our rocket analogy and extend it to a spaceship. Combustion of rocket fuel (adrenaline) is needed for the launch. It's also crucial for the captain of the spaceship (or space shuttle) to know how to direct it once it's airborne, and to know the course to the destination. You wouldn't put a child or a civilian in charge of that spaceship. But the captain has a plan and knows how to do an equipment check, look at all the systems, make sure there is enough fuel for the journey, get back to Earth, and land safely. The same type of checklist applies for public speaking: know why you are there (your intention and your destination); know your crew (know your audience and what's important to them), know your equipment (your voice, your body language, eye contact, environment, and literal equipment, if any); plan for the length of the trip (how long is the speech, and what will you need to have with you throughout the journey?); and know exactly how you are wrapping up (getting home and landing).

I think it's fair to say that most spaceship journeys are not about the captain taking a joy ride or seeking accolades. These journeys take place in hopes of benefiting all of humankind in some way. Aim to make your public-speaking journey a way to be of service, to help others to grow and learn, and to touch the hearts and minds of people with new ideas and new inspiration.

Get Busy

If you focus on being of service, you won't have a lot of time to think about screwing up because you'll be too busy trying to think of ways to help your audience learn something, get inspired, or consider new ideas. You could get up in front of a room and give a flawless speech, but if the audience doesn't leave with something of value, they won't think it was a very good presentation. However, even if you stumble or lose your place, the audience will remember and appreciate you for giving them knowledge, motivation, or inspiration. They probably won't even remember the mistake. They'll just think you were terrific because you gave them something they could actually use to make their jobs or lives better.

Come Bearing Gifts

Think of a presentation as a gift, a *present*-ation that you give to help improve others' lives in some way. If it's a sales presentation, set your mind on helping your audience reach their goals, not on selling your product or idea.

- Always focus on creating more value. What will your audience gain? Your audience is always tuned in to WIIFM—*What's in it for me?* You've got to know that and focus on that.

- Remember the saying "People don't care how much you know until they know how much you care." Don't try to impress them. Aim to help them.

- You must be convinced without a shadow of a doubt in your message, product, or service. If you don't believe in your product, service, or idea, no one else will, either. If you feel that this presentation is just your job, or a necessary evil and you are just going through the motions, your audience will feel that way, too.

- Hold yourself to your own personal high standards and give your best to everything you do.

Desensitized Calmfidence

When I was hosting my first local call-in show in New Jersey, we only went live on the air once a month. Every month it felt like I was starting over. The first half hour I was nervous and rusty, and the second half hour I would find my comfort zone and my rhythm, and relax and enjoy. But then a whole month would pass, and I wasn't able to get desensitized to the nerves or find my footing. This is why public speaking is so hard for most people—because they don't have to do it every day. They don't get used to it. And because the events are so far and few between, and the times you do it seem so nerve-wracking, you may associate only negative feelings with it. My confidence only began to increase as I went on-air weekly, then daily. Constantly doing the thing you fear eventually conquers the fear.

I deliberately had my son get up in church beginning at the age of seven to stand at the podium and read passages into the microphone in front of a room of two hundred or more people to get him desensitized. He was too young to have established a fear of public speaking yet or to have heard people talk about their fear. Many times, our fear actually comes from other people's stories! I didn't force him. I made it sound like fun. I would do readings as well, so he felt that we were taking turns.

Now he has no problem speaking in front of a class or any fear of public speaking at all. The strange truth about fear is that when you face it, the fear quickly goes away. Chip away at your fear. Work through it. The more you do anything, the easier it gets.

No Passion/No Energy = No Audience

A public-speaking secret is that you must have sincerity, emotion, and enthusiasm. You've got to believe wholeheartedly in what you're saying. You have to be incredibly enthusiastic about it, and you have to really want it to benefit the audience.

- You have to *feel and live* the thing that you're trying to speak about. Enthusiasm can banish doubts, negative self-talk, and fear.

- Enthusiasm needs to be heard and seen, especially in our facial expressions, body language, and voice energy. They all have to be in sync, telling the same story.

- You must truly feel enthusiasm before you can possibly verbally or nonverbally express it.

- If you've been assigned a topic that you don't find very exciting, you have to do whatever it takes to find the passion and enthusiasm in your topic—if not for yourself, for your audience. Think about why this is important to them.

Find the Love

Find a reason to like your audience. Even better, find a reason to *love* your audience. You've got to be in this experience together. We all have being human in common. An audience will mirror your energy, emotion, and your vibe. Love yourself, love humanity, love your audience. I believe the number-one key to public-speaking Calmfidence is to be WITH your audience, not separate from them. Now, this doesn't mean that you need to physically walk among them (although it's wonderful if you actually can) but that you need to truly be with them in your approach, your intention, and your energy. Know their needs and concerns. Think of yourself as one of them, not a removed disconnected entity in front of them. Look for ways to relate, speak their language, walk in their shoes. Have a discussion, a conversation. No one wants to be presented at. Don't just push out information. Pull them in with stories, analogies, and metaphors. Find ways to enjoy being among them. Be in the moment with them. When you feel connected to your audience, your Calmfidence will increase, and so will your credibility.

Picture This

Visualize your speech going well. See everything falling into place smoothly. Envision yourself succeeding and your audience enjoying it. It's amazing how easily and vibrantly we can visualize what can go wrong, what we don't want to have happen, how we don't want to feel. People are so good at this that their bodies even start responding: their heart pounds, they sweat, and they get nauseous, dizzy, and terrified just thinking about it—and it's not even happening yet! Visualization is very effective, so why not use it to your advantage? It only makes sense that we can do the exact opposite as well. Make yourself visualize the presentation only in a positive light. See yourself stepping up in front of your audience; see the strong, knowledgeable, and helpful speaker that you wish to be. Watch the whole presentation going well in your mind's eye—right through to the Q&A and complimentary feedback you receive at the end. This will program your subconscious in a powerfully positive way.

The mind does not know the difference between what we visualize in vivid detail and actual performance. If you do this positive visualization exercise several times before a presentation, your subconscious will be on autopilot and will help your conscious mind work the good plan that you have programmed in. Great athletes use this type of visualization all the time. Do you think if they thought about missing a shot they would ever make it?

Preparation

Your audience is more than willing to meet you halfway. They want you to succeed. No one wants to sit through a terrible presentation. They want it to be good. They'll forgive your flaws, mistakes, or missteps, but they will not forgive you if you are unprepared. As the speaker, you need to be the rock in the room. Aim to know more about your subject than anyone else in the room. Know enough to hold your own. Have gravitas, but not in a cocky way. Know your stuff well enough that you trust yourself. Know it well enough that you can rely on yourself to make this work—even if it's not perfect. It can work even if things don't always go as planned. It's the same with Calmfidence: if you wait until the last minute to prepare that speech, speak your mind, or find your courage, you may not have enough time to muster it up on demand. Take time to prepare. As the good old advice goes: dig your well before you're thirsty.

Take Note

I've found that the best way to prepare for a speech or presentation is to first decide what your main goal is. What do you want or need your audience to take away from the time they will spend with you? Then work on the main content. Don't worry about how you will start the speech or how you'll wrap up just yet. Decide how many topics or sections you need to discuss. Then do a brain-dump draft for each area you need to talk about. Edit and fine-tune each section you have. Then put them together in logical order.

Now that you have the body of your speech, read it through a few times in its entirety. Make any additional changes that may surface. Now you'll have a better handle on the big picture of your presentation. Write your opening based on how you want to introduce the content you now have. Start with a story that will stir some kind of emotion—this is one of the best ways to begin. Then write the closing to sum up everything, reinforce important takeaways, and tell your audience how they can put what you've presented into use once they leave.

Now you have a full script from open to close. But you're not done yet. If you take this script as is and present it to your audience, you'll have to read it off the page. You'll be looking down and not making eye contact with the people you are talking to. You'll look and sound scripted. It will be impossible to sound conversational and in the moment. So how can you prevent this?

It's time to reverse-engineer and turn everything you have into bullet points on note cards. This might sound terrifying at first, but by the time you do this you will have internalized much of the information you worked on in the body of your speech. You will understand and know your concepts. This is why you should never procrastinate preparing for a presentation. A sure-fire way to overcome public speaking anxiety is to feel that you are prepared. Avoid the trap of waiting until the last minute. Procrastination will make your public-speaking fears come true.

Write in clear, large print. Number each of your cards in case you drop them or they get shuffled out of order. Turn your full script into a skeletal form of your script with your own personal shorthand, key words, and titles to prompt you through your discussion. This way you can just glance down, grab a point, bring it up, and talk to your audience about it. You'll put the flesh and fat back on that skeletal structure with your conversation discussing those bullet points. If you practice this, you'll have more flexibility while coming across as conversational, in-the-moment, authentic, and personable.

Oh No! I Have to Speak HOW Long?

Another one of my media-training clients is a talented home-decorating expert. We worked together may times preparing him for three- to four-minute television appearances. He was used to preparing a few points and tips. TV interviews are quick little morsels, and most clients need to fine-tune their talking points to fit these fast-moving segments. He was good at it and always had fun going on the air. Then he was asked to give a half-hour presentation on home décor for a website program, and he panicked. *How am I possibly going to fill so much time all on my own without an interviewer asking questions?* he thought.

I suggested he break this down into chunks of time instead of thinking of the entire half hour. I had him pick three main topics that he wanted to focus on. We gave them each about ten minutes. Now we broke it down further. What three things could he talk about in each of those three topics? We allotted three minutes to chat about each of those subtopics. Suddenly he was worried he didn't have ENOUGH time! (Here's the math: 3 x 3 = 9 and 9 x 3 = 27.) So now we were at twenty-seven minutes, with three minutes of time left to fill. His introduction and wrap-up could be a minute-and-a-half each. Suddenly he had his full half hour! He nailed it and they loved him.

Get Ready for Your Close-Up

It's time to videotape yourself. Review your bullet points. Don't think of your preparation as memorization. Think of it as internalizing your content and getting a strong handle on the concepts you want your audience to grasp and understand.

Make an outline, like a table of contents that you can glance down at, and then simply talk about each point and section. Because you know it inside and out, the bullet points should be there to prompt you with your main points so that you can have a more organic conversation with your audience.

Now get yourself a video camera and a tripod. Digital cameras are easy to find and very affordable these days, and odds are good that one of your friends or a family member has one you can borrow. Or, get a tripod for your cell phone.

Practice your bullet-point presentation a few times and then videotape yourself. It's probably best if you do this alone. You might feel silly, but you're the only one who's going to see this. Make sure you record yourself in a wide shot so that you can see your body from head to toe. Try to do a minimum of three to five minutes of presenting. Don't look right into the camera but have it facing you. Pretend that you're speaking to an audience in the room, and try to forget the camera is even there if you can.

Now play it back. Watch it a few times. Here's what you should be looking for: Do you look happy to be there? Are you enthusiastic? Do your facial expressions match the words that you're saying? What's your body language saying?

Watch it again and, this time, turn the sound off. Really watch your face. Is it telling the same story as your words? Now turn the sound back on. Does your voice sound strong, or weak?

By doing this over and over you will begin to see your strengths and weaknesses. You can make adjustments and experiment with both your verbal and nonverbal communication skills. Try to watch yourself from an outside perspective. Don't be a harsh critic. Cut yourself some slack and know this is a process. Look for things you like and things you'd like to improve or change. If you're nervous or new to presenting, odds are that you are speaking too fast. Know this going in. Take a deep breath before you start. Don't focus on the length of your speech. Take one line, one section at a time. Let your audience digest it. Some people rush because they don't want to take up too much of their audience's time. But if you rush, your audience will miss most of what you are saying and you will have wasted their time.

Minimize Distracting Habits

YOU KNOW, YOU KNOW?

Are you a *You Know*-er? Unfortunately, many people are today. I think people feel it's become part of casual conversation, but it's a bad habit. As my father always said, "If we *knew*, we would not need you to tell us." When this phrase is used repetitively in a short period of time, it makes a person sound nervous, immature, and unsure of themselves. Several years ago, a high-profile contender for a political position appeared as a guest on a local New York news program. Perhaps she was nervous, uncomfortable, or unprepared, but this poor woman must have said "you know" more a hundred times during the sit-down interview with the reporter. I believe it damaged her credibility because she just didn't come across as direct and concise in her statements. She was not in command of her own voice and presence, and she didn't get the job. The best way to prevent *you know*s from coming up during a presentation or an interview is to stop saying them in your everyday conversation. Start noticing when other people say it, too. It will really start to drive you crazy, and you'll start avoiding it yourself. If you get rid of the habit in your everyday conversation, you will be less likely to say *you know* during interviews and presentations.

RIGHT?

In an attempt to engage and seek agreement from another person, some people have the bad habit of saying *right?* after a statement, as if to get immediate understanding or approval from the person they are speaking to. But it's annoyingly overused and can sound condescending. If they agree that you're right, they will say so.

SPRAYING VERBAL GRAFFITI

Um, uh, ah, er, uh. You've heard them all. You've probably sprayed some yourself. "Verbal graffiti" is the happy little phrase used to describe those filler words and sounds that we use when we're afraid of dead air or when we're compelled to just keep talking when we're unsure of exactly what we want to say. Verbal graffiti kicks into high gear the faster we speak. I've been a member of the Screen Actors Guild/American Federation of Television and Radio Artists for over twenty years and lucky enough to appear in national commercials, film, and television. I've seen my share of scripts and can tell you that verbal graffiti is usually written into scripts when the character is going to be portrayed as nervous, unprepared, uncomfortable, confused, or uneducated. So, it's important to keep it to a minimum when you are giving a speech—and, for that matter, when speaking anytime to anyone. Here's how:

- One of the best ways to minimize verbal graffiti is, first, to be aware that you have the habit. Videotape or audiotape yourself speaking or have a friend or family member interview you. Play it back and listen.

- You can also ask friends and family if they notice you filling in spaces with *um*s and *ah*s. Ask them to point it out or tap you on the arm each time they hear one.

- Slow down. Take your time. Know that you're most likely going to speak fast, especially if you're nervous, and remind yourself that you need to go slower.

- Don't speed up because you feel like you don't want to take up people's time. Don't go fast just to "get it over with."

- Aim to accept brief moments of silence.

- Replace filler words with a pause instead.

Know that pausing is a sign of intelligence. It shows that you are considering all the facts, processing information, or trying to correctly recall information for accuracy.

THE LOW TALKER

I recently attended a presentation in a hotel conference room to hear a famous sports coach speak about his training and motivation techniques. I had watched a documentary on him and purchased several of the many books he had written. I must admit I was a little obsessed and super excited to finally get to hear and see him in person. To my surprise and dismay he was a low talker! I was up front in the second row and still struggled to hear what he was saying. The hotel staff came in several times and turned up the volume on the sound system, but the problem was that he had a mellow speaking style and was not holding the microphone close enough to his chin. He kept the microphone down by his chest and spoke softly—nothing the staff did helped. He had golden information and fascinating stories to share, but we all had to work so hard to try to hear him that I started giving up and tuning out. I could tell that others in the audience felt the same as a restless energy filled the room. To make matters worse, even though he was holding his microphone, he stayed locked behind a podium that served as a barrier between us. This went on until it was time for a break.

At the break, I approached one of his associates to ask if they could tell him to hold the microphone up closer to his chin. Their answer surprised me. They told me he didn't like using a microphone! As my eyes widened I told them while that might be the case, no one in the room could hear him and people were starting to leave, so they better tell him. When the break was over he did start off holding the microphone closer to his mouth, then quickly dropped back into the old position—and we all again struggled to hear him . Here was a situation where I eagerly wanted to hear everything this man had to say, yet I found myself wondering how long I had to sit through this pain.

Imagine if your audience isn't as excited as I was to see this guy in the first place. Don't make your audience have to work so hard to hear you. Keep in mind that people naturally tune in and out, thinking of other things, as they listen to even the best speakers. Attention spans are getting shorter and shorter with the way we receive and digest information in a digital world. If you can't hear the speaker well, you will almost completely take a mental exit as you sit through the speech, hoping the end is near.

DON'T BE CHEAP WITH YOUR SMILE

Did you smile at the start or finish of your presentation? Have you smiled at all? As I've already said a few times in this book, people who are nervous, unprepared, or lack Calmfidence don't smile. If you are prepared and know your stuff and you still don't smile, you will send the wrong message to your audience. They will see you as unapproachable, unwelcoming, or lacking emotional intelligence. Show them you are happy to be there.

QUIRKS AND JERKS

Look to see if you have any distracting habits, such as adjusting your eyeglasses a lot, fixing your hair with your hand, or tossing your head to fling your hair back. If your hair tends to hang in your face, you need to spray it or gel it before your talk, so you don't fuss with it during your presentation.

Do you grimace or get a mean look on your face when you concentrate? Do you lick your lips a lot or bite them? Do you wring your hands or rub your fingers together? So many of these unconscious habits and pacifiers draw more attention to your nervousness. Half the battle of fixing a distracting habit is realizing that you have it in the first place. This is why videotaping yourself is so valuable.

Do Your Body Language Check

Revisit chapter 13, "Body-Language Calmfidence," and look at your body language. Are you slouching, pacing, rocking, clasping your hands, or holding on to your pen for dear life? Remember that posture is your first communicator. Get used to standing up straight, balanced on both feet. People like symmetry, and an audience will like you more when you stand up straight and don't lean to one side.

The most open and appealing place to keep your arms is straight down, loosely by your sides. Feel free to move around and use gestures. Remember to not clasp your hands or put them in your pockets or behind your back. When hands are clasped together it prevents natural hand gesturing and kills energy and flow. Hands clasped tight read as stress.

One CEO I coached wanted to keep both hands in his pockets while he was giving a PowerPoint presentation, which made him look like he was wearing a straitjacket. It made him twist his whole body from side to side since he could not gesture with his hands. He told me he was trying to look casual and relaxed. When I showed him what it looked like on video he was shocked.

As I mentioned previously, people who are nervous or stressed tend to shove their hands into their pockets. Wouldn't it be terrible to unintentionally send a message like that when we thought we were trying to look calm and casual?

Unfortunately, we are often conditioned to stand in a protective, defensive, or introverted manner and don't even know it. People get used to blocking and covering their torsos with crossed arms, or leaning up against a wall or table, rather than just standing up straight and tall. You will look strong and approachable if you keep your body language open and don't hide your hands or hold onto objects as crutches.

The Calmfidence Stance

Picture two glasses of water on a table. One is tall and skinny; the other is short and wide. Now picture that you bump into that table. Which glass is most likely to fall over? I coach my clients and students to stand solidly on the ground, feet apart, flat on the floor with good posture when giving a speech or standing in front of a camera presenting. I ask them to imagine that their feet are like the roots of a strong oak tree. It's hard for some people to stand this way. Some clients want to cross their ankles in an X shape while standing. Others like to point their toe up and twist on their heel as they speak. Then there's the person who paces like they are waiting for a baby to be born. Others put their weight on one hip and slouch to the side or put one foot in front of the other, as if they are about to take off in a race. All of these stances can cause people to lose their balance, lose their symmetry, leak energy through unnecessary movement, and not feel grounded. Creating a solid foundation from the bottom up is important. Keep your feet slightly separated, about a shoulder width apart. Stand tall and straight but not stiff. You will look and feel surefooted.

It's Just a Conversation

Novelist Philip Pullman said, "After nourishment, shelter, and companionship, stories are the thing we need most in the world." I think the word *presentation* should be stricken from the English language! No one wants to be presented at, but we all love it when someone just talks to us, or better yet, tells us a good *story*.

Any presentation, formal or informal, should be a *human* conversation that you are having with a *human* audience. They want to feel that you are genuine and approachable, and just talking things over with them. It doesn't matter how serious or official the topic may be. There is always a way to tap into the human aspect of how what you have to say relates to the lives of the people you are talking to.

When I was anchoring live breaking news or medical and financial corporate media, as serious as they could be, I still strove for ways to keep my delivery very real and conversational, and I tried to tap into whatever human element I could find. People just want you to talk to them. Think of how we learned as children in elementary school. Who didn't love story time? Whether it was someone reading to us or showing us a film or video, it seemed more like a fun break than a teaching session, didn't it? So, think of yourself as a good storyteller and conversationalist. Think of how you have conversations with family, friends, and coworkers. Isn't there always some storytelling involved? You can become a good storyteller and conversationalist in your public speaking as well, if you make it your intention and your practice. There are really only two ways to share your knowledge. You can push it out to people, or you can pull them in with a story. What's your story?

Get Technical

CASE THE JOINT

Find out in advance about the environment of the room where you'll be speaking. Check out the location ahead of time if possible, or arrive early. I recently had to give a speech in another state in a hotel conference room. I looked on the hotel's website to view some pictures of its conference rooms. Doing so gave me a better feel for the place, helped me choose what to wear based on the background wall color (don't want to blend into the background and wear the same color as the wall, now, do you?), and made me feel like I had been there before. The result was an instant boost in my comfort level before I even stepped on the plane.

IS THIS THING ON?

I really dislike microphones that are attached to podiums because the podium acts as a barrier between you and your audience. It doesn't allow you to move around and work your space; but sometimes we have no choice and have to stand behind one. If you are locked into a podium, you may want to increase the energy of your gestures and bump up your verbal and facial story-telling skills to compensate for the barrier of the podium. People tend to get all official and presenter-ish just due to the formality that a podium lends itself to. Try not to let that happen to you. There are admittedly some good things about podiums if you are still finding your comfort zone with public speaking. They can hide shaky legs and make you feel less exposed. You can rest your notes on top of them and keep some water there to help with any cottonmouth.

Aim to get out from behind that podium if possible. Movement also helps to get rid of some of that adrenaline that might be flowing. Feeling separate from your audience can also be more intimidating than feeling like you are together with them. If you encounter a microphone attached to a podium, find out if it's possible for you to remove the microphone from its dock and use it as a handheld microphone so that you can move around. If it's locked in place, you'll want to position it close to your mouth so that you can speak directly into it. But you don't want to look like you're eating it like an ice cream cone. This will cause a loud popping sound when you say words that begin with *p* or *b*.

Don't let a large microphone block your face from the audience—adjust it so it is not standing straight up. If it's small, make sure you position it so that you don't have to crouch to talk into it and your head can be up and facing the audience, not looking down at your notes.

Ask in advance if you can be given a handheld microphone or a lavaliere, which is a small microphone that attaches to your lapel or collar. It looks like the microphones you see news anchors and television hosts wearing. The optimal audio situation is a wireless microphone (either a handheld or lavaliere) that allows you to walk around freely as you talk with your audience. You can work your stage or speaking area and position yourself to take turns speaking in the direction of different sections of your audience. This comes across as inclusive and interactive, allowing you to connect with your audience.

A SOUND IDEA

All sound systems are different. Some hotels, conference rooms, and other venues have lousy audio quality. I highly recommend that you arrive early the day of your speech, or the night before, and do an audio check so that you can hear what your voice sounds like in the room. Have someone stand in the back of the room to be sure they can clearly hear you. It also helps you to hear yourself ahead of time so that how you sound to yourself is not a shock when you start to speak in front of the audience. If it is not possible to do a test run ahead of time, just do your best to get close to that microphone and *project*. You can always ask the audience during your talk if the people in the back of the room can hear you.

If you won't have a microphone for some reason, check out the size of the room and decide how much you'll have to project so that the people farthest from you can hear you. Hopefully it's a presentation to a small group in a small room. It will make you feel better to stand in that space ahead of time and get comfortable in the room by yourself first as well.

Another great reason to be there early is so you can meet and greet the audience as they come in one or two at a time. This is a lot less intimidating than standing up in front of them for the first time as a group. It also gives you a chance to build rapport, and maybe get some further insight into how you can help them and learn about what they hope to get out of the presentation.

Handling a Hostile Audience

The best way to begin a speech to a potentially difficult audience is to immediately get to the point and call out the elephant in the room. What is the thing that is making them potentially contentious in the first place? You need to know your audience, understand their concerns, and know what their needs are. If it's bad news or something controversial, don't delay talking about it or you'll only get them more agitated and annoyed. Getting right to it will establish your credibility and show that you are there to serve your audience's interests, not your own. Never be defensive. Try to appeal to a shared goal. Even in the most contentious situations you can find some kind of agreement on a broader goal that everyone shares. Start with that goal in mind and take it from there. When you immediately grab their attention by letting them know that "you get it," they'll be more likely to want to hear the rest of what you have to say and give you the chance to say it.

DEALING WITH PICKLE PUSSES AND POKER FACES

So, you're on a job interview or speaking in front of a group of people, and a few faces look blank, bored, judgmental, or downright sour. Or you need to deal with someone you don't know, and the look on their face could stop a small army from advancing. Before you make a decision based on what you see, stop and think for a minute—don't judge. So often when people are deep in thought, listening intently, or simply somewhere else in their minds, their facial expressions can be misleading—what we in the business call a pickle puss.

Some people's neutral face can look thoroughly intimidating, yet it's just the way they look when they are not smiling or deep in thought. Several years ago I was on a job interview to be a brand spokesperson, a position I really wanted. The woman who was interviewing me was stone-faced (a.k.a. poker-faced). She was so serious and intense during our interview. Surprisingly, I ended up landing the job. Later she told me she acts that way when she finds someone she is very interested in and has gone into her decision-making mode.

Keep these tips in mind when you are dealing with pickle pusses and poker faces:

- The person may be in the middle of a mental exit. They are someplace else in their mind, maybe thinking about an argument at home, about something else they have to do, or just a million miles away.

- You can bring people back into the moment by asking them a question or making a comment. You could be the thing they need to cheer them up or get their mind off of something.

- The person might be seriously considering investing in you in some way or hiring you.

- They just might be intently listening to you because they are really digging what you are saying, they're learning, or wanting very much to understand you.

- This person might just not be comfortable in his or her own skin and doesn't interact with people very well.

- People will often follow your lead and mirror your attitude and energy. If you approach them with a smile and genuine interest, they may suddenly turn around and surprise you.

- Some people just have poker faces; they can't help it, so don't judge them for their overt lack of expression.

- Finally, be the initiator. Sometimes people are just so glad someone broke the silence, eased an awkward moment, or seemed interested enough to acknowledge them with genuine interaction.

Trust That You Are Ready

When it's time for your presentation, don't overthink it. Trust that you have done your homework and that you are prepared, and let it unfold. As you begin, stand tall, look prepared, plant yourself, make eye contact, pause, smile, and begin.

It's a Wrap! Put a Bow on It!

Okay, so everything is going pretty well, but now you've got to wrap things up and finish. Many people don't know how to gracefully wrap up and close smoothly. As I said earlier, your presentation is a present that you give to your audience. In the end you'll want to wrap it up with a nice big bow by recapping your main points and then telling the audience the next steps they will need to do so they can take action and use what you have given them.

Keep in mind that no matter how long your presentation is, what you say last will be remembered most. Use the good old rule of three's: most people remember three things easily. Tell them three things they can do or three takeaways that will help them in some way. Then thank them for their time, smile, and be done.

Virtual Calmfidence

Even before the COVID-19 pandemic, more and more people started finding themselves having to present virtually. Presenting through virtual meeting platforms like Zoom, Skype, WebX, and Google brings its own challenges. Many teachers, executives, physicians, and even fitness trainers now find themselves in front of the camera, some reluctantly. Many people struggle to make a personal connection remotely. Here are some tips to find your comfort zone in the virtual zone:

- Make eye contact with the camera lens. It may be a little pinhole at the top of your computer but it is the eyes of your viewer. You want to look directly into the camera as much as possible when you are speaking, and even when you are listening.

- Frame yourself correctly. Place your camera at eye level so that you are looking directly into the camera, not up or down into it. Aim for an inch or two of space above your head in the frame—no more. Others should not be able to see your ceiling.

- Lighting is extremely important to make you look your best and make it easy for people to see you well. Invest in what's called a *ring light*, which is easily found on the internet. Place it directly in front of you, close to your computer camera. It will be the most flattering and affordable light you can use. Do not sit with a window behind you. It will make you look dark.

- Look your best with your hair, makeup, and wardrobe. A virtual meeting is up-close and personal. Be sure to powder your face so you don't look shiny in the light.

- Settle in early before any meeting or session. Check your connection, your framing, lighting, and audio.

- Have a conversation. Do not give a presentation.

- It's okay to ask if others can hear you. Know how to use the mute button.

- Once you are in front of the computer's camera, assume that you are being seen and heard at all times.

- Your facial expressions and body language are very important—review chapters 12 and 13.

- Put the spotlight on your viewers and try to focus more on them than on yourself.

- Focus on what you do best. Teach, instruct, inform, entertain, motivate, inspire.

- Be in the moment fully engaged. Practice active listening.

- Up your energy. You are being seen and heard on a flat two-dimensional screen of a laptop or cell phone and your in-person energy will be cut down by about 50 percent. You need to compensate for that.

- Limit distractions in the room around you.

- Work through the kinks. The more you meet and present virtually, the more it will start to feel like a normal communication situation.

- Keep in mind that virtual meetings are new for most people and everyone is trying to figure this out just like you are.

I've never forgotten what it feels like to be a person who fears public speaking. I often remember quivering in my boots in my college business class. But I'm grateful for having gone through that as it makes me a better coach and trainer. If I can overcome years of fear of public speaking, you can, too. This brings us to the next chapter in our journey, another form of public speaking and one in which an added layer of stress and anxiety comes as it deals with our livelihood and landing that job: "Interview Calmfidence."

Public-Speaking
Calmfidence Takeaways

- All speaking really is public speaking, otherwise you'd be by yourself!

- Mistakes and nerves don't matter to people if you give them something of value.

- Take the focus off of yourself and focus on being of service to your audience. A presentation is a gift that you give to help improve others' lives in some way.

- Nerves make you sharp. They show you have passion. They mean that you care. Just because you are nervous doesn't mean you won't do a good job. Lots of people do great things when they do things in spite of their nerves.

- Remember, none of us likes to be presented at, but we all love it when someone just talks to us like a normal human being having a conversation with us or, better yet, tells us a good story.

- A really interesting thing happens when we stop focusing on ourselves and focus on our audience. We suddenly forget about how our voice sounds, how we look, and how nervous we are. When we are concentrating on others' needs, we are in the Calmfidence zone.

Calmfidence Reflections

List three ways you can be of service and give value in a
public-speaking situation:

_____

_____

_____

List three ways you can be better prepared for speaking of any
kind in public:

_____

_____

_____

What are three ways you can relabel the word *nervous* when it
comes to speaking in public?

_____

_____

_____

List three ways you can practice public speaking to become more
comfortable in advance:

_____

_____

_____

15

Interview
Calmfidence

During a job interview I poured some water into a
glass and it overflowed slightly. "Nervous?" asked the
interviewer. I replied, "No, I always give 110 percent."

Anonymous

I had put an ad on Craigslist for an administrative assistant and was
conducting interviews. At the time I was going by my maiden name,
Murphy, and the first name of Pat. The ad contained a link to my website, which had all the information about me and about my company. It
included pictures and videos. I had set up an appointment via email based
on a résumé submitted by a local woman, Michelle, who seemed to have
the experience I needed. The fact that she lived nearby was a big bonus for
me and, I'm sure, for her.

When I answered the door to let Michelle in, she smiled and said,
"Oh, hello. I'm here for an interview with Mr. Murphy."

I smiled back, a little confused. "There's no *Mister* Murphy here, but
I'm Pat Murphy, the owner of the company," I said.

"Oh, my goodness, I'm so sorry, but when I saw the name Pat Murphy,
I assumed you were a man," she exclaimed.

Keep in mind that my ad contained a link to my website. My website was on my email communications with her. My company name was
searchable in Google and other search engines, and so was I. With just

a click of the mouse she could have known in a split second that I was a woman. But she did not click. How could I expect she would click to go the extra mile in her work for me if she didn't even do it for herself? This interview was not off to a good start for Michelle.

"I'm really sorry that I thought you were a man," Michelle said, as we wrapped up our brief interview. Her qualifications were satisfactory, but I knew I could not offer her the job. The next day another candidate, Dani, arrived to interview. "So nice to meet you, Ms. Murphy. I've been following your Instagram tips and reading your blog. That lemon balm really helped me sleep the other night!" Dani had learned the different types of coaching and training that I do, and she explained how her goals aligned with this type of work. She had dug up things on the web about me that I had forgotten were out there. Dani even knew I love pickles and Halloween. She had gone above and beyond to prepare for the interview, and she set herself up to create instant rapport. She had me at hello. This would be the beginning of a beautiful relationship.

Put Your Best Foot Forward

Most people get really stressed out about the interview process. They feel like they are being judged, observed, analyzed, and compared to others—and yes, they are! How can we deal with all that and feel Calmfidence? First, understand that everyone goes through this at some point, and most people feel exactly the same way you do in this situation. There are a lot of things you can do that will give you a sense of control and knowledge that you are putting your best foot forward. Doing your homework and going the extra mile are the keys to interview Calmfidence. Whether it's a virtual meeting or in person, here's what you can do to prepare yourself for a confident successful interview.

YOU MADE THE FIRST CUT

Remind yourself that if you have been invited for an interview, this means they are interested in you. They want to meet you because something about you or your experience made them feel you might be a good candidate for the job.

CHECK THEM OUT

Find out everything you can about the company before the interview. Read through the company's website and search the Web for information about its industry. Don't get crazy trying to remember too much; just get a general sense of what the company does and what its strengths are. If you know the name of the person who will be interviewing you, type their name into a search engine and see what you can find. Check out their LinkedIn and Facebook profiles—and keep in mind they may do the same. Be sure to do a search engine investigation of yourself and make sure anything that comes up is spic and span. Create a LinkedIn profile if you don't already have one. If you have a Facebook profile, keep it professional during the time you are on a job search. We're all connected somehow, and the world is only getting smaller.

IT GOES BOTH WAYS

Remember that an interview is a two-way street. You're there to make sure that this is the right job for you, too! Use the interview to get the information you need to make sure you'll be happy doing the job and working with them. If you look at it this way, you level the playing field: the mindset *I hope they like me* is balanced with *I hope I like them*.

Prepare questions ahead of time that you'll ask your interviewer. Inquire about the values of the company. How do they stay competitive in their industry? Is there a structured career path at the company? How does your interviewer like working for the company? What is the company most proud of? If it's an in-person meeting, be sure to bring a nice leather folder or binder that has a fresh notepad and pen, iPad or small laptop, and a copy of your résumé, even if you know they've already seen it online, to save them the time of finding it on their desk or bringing it up on their screen. Print it on good paper stock—studies have shown that the thicker the paper, the more weight is given to the information on the paper. Allow them to see that you already have researched the company and prepared some notes. Be it in person or virtual, be sure to let them see you taking notes during the interview.

MOCK THE INTERVIEW

Set up a mock interview with family or friends before your real one. Have a friend or family member read over your information about the company and then play the role of the interviewer. Ask them to throw out some good questions about why you want to work at the company, what your goals are, and what you feel you bring to the table. What are your strengths and weaknesses? Do a search for typical human-resource and hiring manager questions on the Web—many different samples will pop up. This will give you solid "real" material to work with as you are practicing. By doing these mock interviews, you'll feel much more comfortable and prepared for the real thing.

CONTROL HOW YOU ROLL

How you look affects your energy and confidence in both virtual and in-person interviews. Choose your wardrobe carefully to be sure that you not only feel great but also look professionally appropriate—even if the position is a casual one. Aim to look a step above the norm.

- If you can, wear a new suit or outfit that you feel great in. It doesn't have to be expensive—it just has to look good on you, fit well, and most important feel secure on you, and you feel good in it. If you can't buy something new, take your favorite outfit to your local tailor or dry cleaner, and have them give it a once-over for hanging threads, loose buttons, or stains. You could even have new buttons put on for a new look. Get it refreshed and pressed and ready to go.

- For a virtual interview, try to wear solid colors. Medium jewel-tone colors look best on camera. Avoid very dark or white colors and busy patterns. Avoid big dangling or shiny jewelry, which can be distracting on camera.

- Make sure your shoes are in good shape. People notice shoes, and you'll feel good walking in a new or spruced-up pair. Same thing goes for your tote or briefcase.

- Be sure to wear shoes during a virtual interview. You'll have a sturdier energy and feel more grounded if you are in shoes, even when no one can see them.

- Even if you are only seen from the waist up during virtual interviews, always be fully dressed. You may underestimate all that a camera can capture, as some videos that went viral during the pandemic shutdown attest. And it's just better to be dressed for conveying a dynamic energy.

- Get a manicure—it doesn't matter if you're a guy or gal, get a manicure. You'll feel more confident and will look more capable. Interviewers notice things like chewed nails or chipped polish!

- Drink more water. Your skin will look better, and your brain is sharper when you're hydrated.

- Visit the location where you will be interviewing a few days ahead of time, if possible. Check out the parking situation, or time how long it takes to walk there from the nearest transit station; note the entrance to the lobby and any security issues. Be sure you have the proper contact info and identifications to gain entry.

- If you will be driving, be sure to fill your car with gas the night before.

- For a virtual interview, plan your environment at least a day before. Choose a quiet room free from distractions. Make sure your background is clean and simple and not near any windows or harsh lights. As mentioned earlier, ensure that your computer's camera lens will be at eye level, even if this means stacking books or boxes to set the computer on. Test your camera and frame yourself so that you have a medium close-up shot (from the chest up, centered, with about two inches of background above your head). Place a light in front of you. A ring light or soft box light is best. If you don't have this type of light, position a large white poster board behind your laptop, facing you, and bounce a light source off of it for a soft, more flattering lighting effect. Check your internet connection and microphone.

- If you haven't been exercising, start now. Do anything, just get moving again. Any form of exercise, including walking, will help get rid of stress, sharpen your thinking, and make you feel better both physically and mentally. This will help you sleep better at night—including the night before the interview. Just don't exercise late in the evening or it may energize you too close to bedtime and not allow you to get to sleep.

- Limit alcohol and caffeine the week leading up to your interview, longer if you can. Now, I know some of you might be saying, *yeah, right,* but you either want to be at your best or you don't; it's that simple. Avoid caffeine after three o'clock in the afternoon the day before your interview. Avoid alcohol the night before your interview. While alcohol may initially help you fall asleep, the likelihood of broken sleep is high. Alcohol induces a false sleep, and if you wake up in the middle of the night, you may have trouble falling off again. You need a good night's sleep.

- Eat a light dinner early. You don't want to be looking for that antacid later or propping yourself up in bed trying to digest.

- Read something uplifting, knowing that you did all your homework for the interview ahead of time. Cramming the night before makes it hard to sleep restfully. Reading something motivational or funny lets your mind unwind and your eyelids get heavy.

- Drink some chamomile tea or warm milk, if dairy doesn't bother your stomach, before you go to bed; these are both natural sleep inducers.

- Go to bed early. If you find yourself unable to sleep, remember that your body is nonetheless getting rest when it is lying still. Don't put so much pressure on yourself to sleep. If you can't turn your mind off, try to switch your thinking to something that you are looking forward to in the near future: a family vacation, seeing an old friend, going to that restaurant you love, or how you want to organize a part of your house that you would enjoy. Just get your mind on something that has no pressure attached to it. Remember that no one else is in control of your thoughts—you really do have control of the thoughts you allow your mind to entertain. You have the choice to choose to think positively, or not.

OFF TO A GOOD START

The morning of your interview, you have a full tank of gas, your mass transit plan in place, or your virtual environment organized, tested, and ready to go. Your new or updated suit or outfit is pressed and on a hanger ready to go, with shined shoes and a smart briefcase or tote. You've gotten a good night's sleep and have been taking care of yourself for at least the last week. It's now time to really rise and shine.

- Get up early. Give yourself plenty of extra time to have a smooth morning. As your feet hit the floor, say *thank* with the right foot and *you* with the left foot. This will launch you into positivity throughout the day.

- Get moving. Go for a long walk, jump rope, stretch, or do mild calisthenics on your floor. It doesn't matter what, just get your heart rate up, get your blood flowing, and get moving. This will absolutely help your stress level today and sharpen your thinking skills and reaction times. It will also put some great color into your face.

- Refuel your body's engine. Eat breakfast. Studies show that kids who eat breakfast tend to do better in school. It would make sense that this would also work for adults in an interview. Choose foods like blueberries, whole grains, peanut butter, yogurt, oatmeal, or hardboiled eggs; their energy will stick with you for a long time into your day. Eat *before* you get dressed—you don't want to get anything on those crisp, clean clothes.

- Limit the java. A little caffeine can give you a spark, but too much might scatter your thoughts and make you speak too fast. It can even tire you out if your caffeine high tanks during the interview. But take note on excessive caffeine. There was a very creepy study done by NASA where spiders were given cocaine, marijuana, narcotics, and caffeine to see how the drugs would affect them. Surprisingly, the spiders had the most trouble trying to create their intricate webs while jacked up on the caffeine! A little caffeine can kick you into action and give you that alert feeling, but learn what your tipping point is. Know your personal tolerance and where you begin talking too fast, get jittery, or start to experience disorganized thinking. This is the point where you'll spin right out of the Calmfidence zone.

- Beware the milk man. Even if you are not lactose intolerant, dairy makes phlegm, which coagulates around your vocal cords. It can put a fuzzy sweater on your tongue, and a coated tongue makes speaking clearly difficult. Voice-over artists, singers, and stage performers never touch dairy right before a performance. You don't want to have to clear your throat during your interview, which can make you sound unsure and nervous. Milk alternatives like coconut, almond, soy, and rice milk are all great substitutes. Or just drink your tea or coffee black. Add a green apple to your breakfast; voice performers use them to cut the phlegm as well.

- Strategically hydrate. Drink a big glass of water when you wake up. Imagine you've been on a flight for six to eight hours with no water or fluid of any kind. How would you feel? When you wake up after a long night's sleep, you are in a similar state. Drinking a full glass of water as soon as you awaken is the single most energizing thing you can do for your body and mind. When you are properly hydrated before that big meeting, speech, event, or job, you'll be on top of your game, quick thinking, and ready to tackle the world. Being hydrated is incredibly important for brain function.

- Do the "idiot check." Double-check that you have everything you need in your briefcase or tote that you want to bring to the interview—including a copy of your résumé.

- Don't stink it up. Skip the perfume and cologne for an in-person interview. Many people are turned off by (or even allergic to) fragrance. We all react differently to different smells. Smell has been called the sense of memory. You don't want to be wearing the same cologne or perfume that triggers a bad memory for your interviewer. I once heard an executive say that she didn't like a job candidate because he smelled like her ex-husband!

- Feed your brain. On your way to the interview, listen to a motivational audiobook or podcast. This will help you to be in an upbeat, enthusiastic, positive frame of mind. A good motivational audiobook makes you focus on what you want, not what you don't want. It feeds your subconscious with the right stuff. A playlist of your favorite upbeat songs that get you pumped up and in a great mood can do the trick as well.

- Be an early bird. Give yourself extra time to get to the location of your interview. You just never know what could come up in your path on the way there. It's better to arrive early and sit and wait than to be late. But being extremely early is often just as bad as being late: busy people have tight schedules and can really get annoyed when someone shows up before they are ready for them. Wait in your car, in the lobby, down the hall, or, if you have no place to wait other than the reception area, tell the receptionist or first person you encounter that you are early and would just like to wait there before they announce your arrival at the appropriate time.

- If you're doing a virtual interview, don't sit down the minute before the interview is set to begin. Give yourself at least ten minutes to get into your space, turn everything on, and begin reviewing your notes.

GO IN STRONG

For an in-person interview, enter with a firm handshake, strong voice, and positive dynamic energy. For a virtual interview, be sure your energy is up, you log on with a big smile, sit up straight, and make great eye contact with the lens the majority of the time.

TO TELL THE TRUTH

During your interview, avoid saying "to be honest." It's an overused phrase that attempts to let people know you are being upfront and open with them. Hiring managers and interviewers say this is one of the most annoying phrases they hear, and they hear it all too often. I cringe every time I hear it, no matter who says it. It implies that sometimes you're not honest, or you might not have been honest up until now. Alternatives that show you have a calm confidence are "to be open," or "to be candid," which will make you sound more direct, trustworthy, and genuine.

The Telephone Interview

Employers may want to speak with you on the phone before they call you in for an interview or video call. Telephone interviews differ from in-person interviews in many ways that benefit you. You have more control over things. You don't have to worry about your appearance, where you should be looking, what to do with your hands, or expressions your face may be making. You can stay laser-focused on your expertise and experience, and on what your goals are.

BEFORE A CALL

Just as you would for an in-person interview, first learn everything you can about the company and about the person who will interview you. Locate a picture of the interviewer on the web so that you can visualize what they look like when you are having a conversation with them. Print out their picture and keep it on your desk during the interview, if possible, or have it up on your computer screen.

When you agree to the phone interview, ask approximately how long the interview will be—fifteen minutes, half an hour? Who will call whom on what number? Try to arrange a time and place that works best for both of you, not just for them.

MAKE A GAME PLAN

Don't just wing it like it's a casual conversation. Instead, determine three to five key points that you believe make you a great candidate for the job, along with some ideas you might have that can help the company be more successful. If you've done your homework on the company, you may have identified challenges it is experiencing. If not, ask your interviewer to identify some challenges and then propose how you might be able to help resolve them. *Be a problem solver.* The company has a problem and has a job it needs to fill. Think of yourself as a solution to the problem and describe how you can help, whether it's by making more money, saving money, saving time, getting better organized, and so on.

Do a brain dump of all your ideas in advance, writing them out fully. Then rewrite them as a list of bullet points so that you won't sound like you are reading a verbatim script. Referring to these bullet points keeps you sounding conversational as you turn them back into sentence form during the interview.

Know your points inside and out—not memorized but internalized! When you speak, don't go on and on; less is more. Be clear and concise. Don't be afraid of pauses and silence, otherwise you'll be compelled to fill the silence and over-talk. Remember, pauses are a sign of intelligence. They show that you are taking the time to consider the question and provide a thoughtful answer.

DON'T GO IN NAKED!

Just because this is a phone interview doesn't mean that you can be in your crusty PJs, old sweatpants, or, heaven forbid, butt naked! I said earlier that one of the great things about a phone interview is that you don't have to worry about your appearance, but I meant *how you appear to your interviewer*. How you appear to *yourself* is another matter completely.

When we're at home wearing pretty much anything that we wouldn't wear outside of the house except maybe to get the mail, our energy is different, the way we carry ourselves is different, and the way we feel about ourselves may be different. If you've got "bed head" and last night's mascara smudged under your eyes, or stubble on your face, most likely you don't feel so bright-eyed and bushy-tailed.

In order to feel strong, dynamic, and engaging during a phone interview, we need to dress the part for *ourselves*. Just as body language can influence how we feel about ourselves and even change our stress and success hormone levels (refer to the chapter "Body-Language Calmfidence"), the same is true for how we dress our body. So, while you may not have to get all suited up for that phone interview, know that you'll feel stronger if you get your external act together and feel more presentable.

CONSIDER YOUR SURROUNDINGS

- Driving during a phone interview is probably not a good idea. Your attention will always be split between the call and the road.

Hands-free Bluetooth connections don't have the best sound, and you don't want the interviewer struggling to hear you. You're sunk if you hit a dead zone and the call gets dropped.

- Taking the call in a public place like an outdoor park bench or in a busy coffee shop might sound pleasant until horns start blowing, crows start cawing, or someone plops down next to you talking loudly on their phone.

- If you're on an office phone or landline, don't use a speakerphone. You may sound like you're in a tunnel or calling from long distance. It may come across as impersonal. Speakerphones can also give someone the impression that you're doing other things during the call and not giving the interviewer your full attention.

- Turn off call waiting so that you're not interrupted by a succession of annoying beeps. If you're at home, you need to let your roommates or family members know that you need quiet with no interruptions. Minimize the chances of any dogs barking in the background, doorbells ringing, or alarms going off. Shut the door to the office or room where you'll be taking the call.

- If your landline is a cordless phone, be sure it's fully charged. Many times, we let cordless phones hang around the house off their docks—and the time to realize the battery is running low is not when you are about to get on that call or during it.

- Go hands-free if possible, with a headset or ear buds so that you can refer to your notes or write. Be careful not to shuffle papers too much.

- Turn off all radios, televisions, ringers, email alerts, and laptop sounds. Turn computer speakers on tower units down or off.

- It's always a good idea to ask the interviewer at the beginning of the call if they hear you clearly; be sure you can hear them clearly as well.

- If you have to sneeze, cough, or clear your throat during the call, move the phone away from your mouth and neck or mute it.

Swallow water away from the mouthpiece of the phone to avoid gulping sounds. Noises sound so much louder over the phone.

- Get yourself a big glass of water to keep at your desk during the call so you can sip it if you get dry mouth or a scratchy throat. Again, you don't want to have to clear your throat or cough during the call, if possible. Since you'll be staying hydrated, use the restroom before you get on the call.

- Be sure there is some form of a clock nearby so you can judge the length of the call. This way you can gauge when things are wrapping up or if they are keeping you on the phone longer than expected.

- Since you are in the room for the duration of the call, make sure you check what the room temperature will be after you have the door closed for a while. Rooms can get too hot or too cold once the door is shut, especially if it is a door you don't normally keep shut.

CHEAT SHEETS AND NOTES

One of the best things about telephone interviews is that you can have an arsenal of material around you that you can refer to during the call and no one else but you will see it. Have a copy of your résumé in front of you, and your bio if you have one. Clear the desk area or surface you will be at of anything that doesn't relate to the interview so you can avoid shuffling around to find stuff when you're in the middle of the call.

Have a sheet of questions that you want to ask about the job and the company. Write out those three to five key points that you believe make you a great candidate for the job and some ideas you have of ways you can help them.

Have a list of questions you hope they won't ask you, and create short answers for them ahead of time. You need to be prepared even if you don't want to go there. Also have what you consider no-brainer information in front of you. This is basic information that should be on the tip of your tongue that you think you would never forget. It would be embarrassing if you blanked on it during an interview.

Have the company website displayed on the screen of your computer for reference. Check for news about the company's industry the morning of your interview to avoid the interviewer knowing more about current information than you do.

CREATE A SUCCESS INDEX CARD

Just like the Calmfidence credit card I talked about in the chapter "Calm-fidence Tools," your "Success" index card will remind you at a quick glance just how wonderful you are!

We often forget about many of our successes and the great feedback we've received over the years. Just like the performer who agonizes over one bad review among twenty-five good ones, we don't focus enough on what has *gone right*. Worse, we minimize it. Brainstorm in advance of any phone interview (or any form of a job interview, for that matter) and write down every big and small success at work that you've had over the past several years—even stuff you think is trivial—just get it all down on paper. Then dig up any complimentary reviews, notes, emails, feedback, even verbal feedback you can remember, and get it all out there in front of you. If you've never taken this kind of inventory before, it's usually an eye opener.

Next, take what you think is the cream of the crop, five or six items that you feel great about, and write them down as bullet points on an index card. Have the card prominently on your desk. It should be the very last thing you look at before you get on that call or go into an in-person interview. It's a great thing to keep in your briefcase or pocketbook for future reference anytime you need a boost or reminder.

VOICE, ENERGY, AND DELIVERY

Your voice is all they've got to go on during a phone interview. They can't see your body language or your facial expressions. You can't give them a nice strong handshake or flash that gorgeous smile of yours. Your voice is the star of the show. Your energy, passion, Calmfidence, and expertise all have to be wrapped up into one big ball of dynamic verbal communication skills.

When I do voice work for commercials, movies, training videos, and news reports, I always stand up in front of the microphone. Standing makes your voice sound better. You're not crunching your diaphragm. Your breathing will flow better. Your energy is up. There's more movement and life. When you stand, your voice will sound strong, calm, and confident. Make the desk or area you are speaking from standing-room friendly so that you can get access to everything from a standing position and have room to casually move about during the call. This way you also will not be locked into place. If you have to sit for some reason, then be at the edge of your seat, in a powerful posture, ready for action. Don't cave into yourself or into the chair.

The first thing I do when I coach a client for phone interviews, whether they are for job interviews or media interviews, is to see how the client handles the initial hello. The first line or two that you speak sets the tone for the conversation. Your voice should be bright, upbeat, enthusiastic, welcoming, and strong. Many people don't turn it on until they get into the conversation. This is a mistake. Those first lines are your first impression. The interviewer will be thinking either *This is going to be a good interview* or *This is going to be like watching paint dry.*

When I have interviewed people over the phone as a reporter, I can tell right away if our conversation is going to be upbeat and interesting or hum-drum. When I get a dynamic voice on the other end of the phone, it makes me want to conduct a better interview. Be sure you are projecting loud and clear; don't make the interviewer have to work hard to hear you and interact with you.

Even though the person on the other end of the line can't see your face, smile when you say hello and anytime you are offering information that is solution-oriented or recapping accomplishments. A smile changes your energy and the sound of your voice. Customer-service trainers teach their employees to smile when talking to customers over the phone because people can *hear* the smile in your voice.

Watch your pace; speed is a telltale sign of nerves. Don't confuse a brisk pace with passion and enthusiasm. If you tend to speak fast when you get nervous or excited, which many people do, you need to remind yourself to slow down.

Don't end sentences with an upward inflection. Always bring your register down at the end of each sentence. This will keep statements from sounding like questions and will make you sound more definite and surefooted. Women tend to use this upward inflection more often and can easily end up speaking in high C. Engage those stomach muscles when you speak, as if you were doing a crunch. Your voice should be coming from deep in your belly, not from high in your throat or nasal area.

Be dynamic. Know your value. Speak from a place of experience, know-how, and high personal standards.

Really listen. Think about the question and take a moment to give a thoughtful answer. This will help to minimize those *likes, ums, ers, ahs,* and *ya knows*. Warm up your voice prior to the call. Practice a few answers out loud. You can even sing! Singing gets your voice moving and can put you in a positive frame of mind. Just as when you record your outgoing voice mail you re-record it a few times before you are satisfied, do this with a few answers out loud before you get on the phone call.

OTHER POWER TIPS

- Avoid eating right before your interview. Almonds and nuts are a disaster. They get stuck in your teeth and caught in your throat. I crack up every time I see them at the snack table in TV and production studios. I know some TV guest experts who learned the hard way to avoid them right before going on the air.

- Never say, "That's a good question." This is more of a habit than anything else, and it's a known stall tactic. It can also sound as if you didn't think their other questions were good. It's better to say: "I'm glad you asked that question." It helps if you really are glad that they asked that question.

- Use your notes! No one is watching in a phone interview. But stay focused on what you're being asked.

- Speak in sound bites, golden nuggets, and tight little morsels.

- Stay focused. Without a person in front of you, it's easy to let distractions creep in.

- Don't talk about the weather. It's an overused conversation starter. The only exception is if a storm is a major news story or something truly worthy of talking about.

- Always stay upbeat and positive, no matter what. Enjoy the opportunity. Savor it and have fun.

When we put ourselves out into the spotlight communicating to others, whether it's for a job interview, a television interview, virtually, or for an in-person public speaking presentation, there is so much we can do to get mentally and physically prepared to be calm and confident when we feel like we are being observed, critiqued, and even judged. But sometimes we need an extra trick or remedy to help us calm down, get focused, and feel our best. This brings us to part 4 of our journey, where we'll discuss some of nature's secrets to boost our Calmfidence naturally.

Interview Calmfidence Takeaways

- You've been invited to be interviewed because someone thinks you are a good candidate for the job.
- Go the extra mile on homework and research.
- Remember that you are interviewing them as well.
- Get your mind, body, spirit, and environment in top shape ahead of time.
- Don't take phone interviews casually or less seriously than in-person interviews.
- Avoid certain foods and habits that can derail your success.
- Create your Success index card.

Calmfidence Reflections

List three kinds of research on the company and the interviewer(s) you can do prior to your interview:

_____

_____

_____

How will you get your presentation content into good shape?

_____

_____

_____

What can you do to get yourself into top physical, mental, and emotional shape leading up to your interview?

_____

_____

_____

What are three ways you can control your environment during a telephone interview?

_____

_____

_____

List five items you can include on your Success index card:

_____

_____

_____

_____

_____

Part Four

Natural Calmfidence

16

Natural Calmfidence Remedies

The greatest secrets are always hidden
in the most unlikely places.
Roald Dahl

Many clients tell me they take something or have a glass of wine to calm down before a big presentation or event and are ultimately sorry they did. The alcohol may have helped stop their heart from pounding, but they spent the next hour trying to straighten out their head. The wine dulled the adrenaline and nerves that would have made them sharp, and now they didn't trust themselves to be quick on their feet or ready to react and be fully present in the moment. Clients who have taken Xanax before a presentation seem flat and lacking in energy.

Very rarely do drugs and alcohol get you truly calm and clear; they usually just dull the reality of the situation, your judgment, and your reaction time. It's like giving a dog that is afraid of thunder or fireworks a sedative—it's still afraid but its body doesn't react as it expects, which can make the dog feel trapped; some veterinarians advise against medicating for these events. When you're afraid, would you rather know that you are capable of reacting, taking action, and making a move? Or would you rather feel spaced-out, muffled, and glassy-eyed?

True Calmfidence comes from within. If you keep dulling your response and reactions, you cheat yourself of the gift of desensitization and getting to another level of tolerance.

While I have helped thousands of people to develop a quiet inner trust and peace of mind with my behavioral and psychological techniques, it also helps to have a few of nature's little tricks up your sleeve. There's a definite connection between our senses and mood, and over the years I've collected studies and information on the foods, fruits, and herbs and spices that are the most effective in promoting calm and confidence. These tips are not only delicious but also fun to try. Following are some natural remedies that I recommend to all my clients to help them create their inner calm. Always consult with your doctor or healthcare provider if you are currently taking medications, are pregnant or breastfeeding, or have any health concerns before adding any of these foods to your diet.

Fruitful Calmfidence

LEMON BALM IS THE BOMB

When it comes to calm, cool Calmfidence this is probably the tip I most recommend to clients. Lemon balm extract reacts in receptors in the same part of the brain as Xanax and Valium, so it provides relaxation and positive feelings but as a natural alternative to drugs. I know people who use it as a natural sleep aid in tea at night, a few drops under the tongue before a big presentation, and even to deal with the stress and anxiety of medical treatments and their side effects.

LIFE CAN BE LIKE A BOWL OF CHERRIES

Get these plump juicy guys into your diet. I first learned of the calming effect of cherries when visiting an internist specializing in longevity, during a stressful period of my life. I was having trouble sleeping and he suggested I eat cherries, which are naturally high in melatonin, a compound that helps make us sleepy. They really helped (bonus: they are delicious). So, I decided to take it a step further and began blending organic frozen cherries into my smoothies and breakfast shakes and found that I was calmer and managed daily stressors better, too.

GO BANANAS

One of the first performers I coached to help him transition his career from Broadway to television hosting told me that he and fellow cast members rely on bananas to handle their nerves on stage. They swore that bananas acted as natural beta blockers to help minimize the physical reactions of performance anxiety. The potassium and tryptophan contained in bananas can act in the same way as some medications to help minimize anxiety. Bananas have also been shown to act as a natural muscle relaxer, which can help with the physical tension that comes from stress and public-speaking fears.

HAVE A CRUSH ON CITRUS

As a spokesperson for a *Prevention* magazine video series on health and wellness, I learned that simply smelling citrus can cut down on the stress hormone cortisol. Citrus can also help with nausea and digestion, two problems that can plague people with nervous stomachs. Plus, vitamin C is a major antioxidant that helps our bodies to function better in general.

GRAPE EXPECTATIONS

Reports in the *European Journal of Nutrition* show that drinking a cup of Concord grape juice can make you feel calmer in just minutes. The polyphenols in Concord grape juice help to curb the release of the stress hormone cortisol and boost calming GABA (gamma-aminobutyric acid), a naturally occurring amino acid that works as a neurotransmitter in the brain.

REACH FOR SOME LYCHEE

Lychee fruit is rich in polyphenols, which minimize the effects of stress and lower cortisol levels, helping you feel more confident. In addition, studies show a mixture of lychee and green tea can reduce circulating cortisol levels and oppose other physiological effects of stress. This bite-sized sweet Asian fruit comes canned or fresh and even makes a great summer sangria (with or without the alcohol). I've found it in Asian grocery stores and online.

CUCKOO FOR COCONUT WATER

This superhero of B-complex vitamins helps to balance your body's electrolytes so you remain calm. It can help reduce anxiety, improve sleep, relax muscles, and improve circulation. Coconut water contains GABA and, like the grapes, has relaxing anti-anxiety effects. Low potassium levels can increase stress, anxiety, and depression, and coconut water has more potassium than four bananas. It's super hydrating, which will help you think more clearly, feel less fatigued, and help alleviate cottonmouth and coated tongue when you are under pressure or nervous, and contains electrolytes to keep you balanced.

Spicy Calmfidence

CINNAMON CALM

Spice up your motivation and performance while you calm your body and mind with cinnamon. Sure, the scent of cinnamon summons warm memories of holidays or comforting baked goods, but breathing in this scent has also been shown to reduce anxiety levels by as much as 25 percent in just two minutes. A study from Wheeling Jesuit University in West Virginia found that the scent of cinnamon may reduce fatigue, increase alertness, improve cognitive functions like memory and attention span, and even decrease frustration and anxiety. Adding cinnamon to food prevents spikes in blood sugar, helping to improve your mood and sense of calm. Keep cinnamon on hand around your home or office. Potpourri, candles, fresh sticks, tea, and gum will all do the trick. Sprinkle it on your breakfast or latte.

THE CARDAMOM KICK

To increase your overall sense of well-being, call on cardamom. The aroma of this herb has some pretty powerful psychological effects that clear your mind from overthinking and lead to peaceful feelings and better decision making, according to the School for Aromatic Studies in New York City. You can carry cardamom as an essential oil and take a whiff as needed. Or brew cardamom tea or add it to warm milk to unwind the night before a big day. Add a bit of cinnamon for a delicious double dose of Calmfidence.

Blooming Calmfidence

LEVITATE WITH LAVENDER

The scent of lavender has been associated with calm and serenity for centuries. But I hadn't heard about it until I got pregnant. My birthing coach, Pauline Nardella, founder of Birthing Wisdom, advises all expectant mothers to purchase lavender essential oils and creams to help manage stress and worry. I was aiming for natural childbirth, and my son turned out to be just about ten pounds when he finally decided to make his debut. I was sniffing lavender every chance I got! Ever since then when I smell lavender, it brings a sweet, soft, calm sensation to my body, mind, and spirit. It's a mini-vacation from stress anytime.

JAZZ IT UP WITH JASMINE

Researchers have found that the fragrance of jasmine flowers can create a sense of alertness, calm your nerves, and lift your mood with feelings of Calmfidence, optimism, and revitalized energy. Studies also show that the scent of jasmine in your bedroom can lead to deeper sleep.

KEEP A STASH OF ASH

Call on the power of ashwagandha when you need to stimulate brainpower, improve your mood, and reduce stress and anxiety in short-term situations. This powerful ancient herb is in same family as the tomato. It has a red fruit about the size of a raisin, oval leaves, and yellow flowers and can be taken as a supplement, a liquid, or a powder added to your favorite smoothie or shake. Ashwagandha is known to help alleviate symptoms of fatigue, improve energy, and increase concentration while providing a general sense of well-being. It can help to improve learning, memory, and reaction time. You can find ashwagandha at your favorite health food store or online.

GET WITCHY

Witch hazel is a shrub with fragrant yellow, pink, or purple flowers. For many years, an astringent lotion has been made from the bark and leaves of this plant. Makeup artists often apply it before they apply makeup to help minimize a sweaty "T-Zone," the area on the face from the center of your forehead, down around the sides of your noise, to your chin just under your bottom lip, where skin tends to sweat and shine the most. Both men and women can use topical witch hazel to prevent looking sweaty and nervous.

I also advise male clients who sweat a lot to carry blotter sheets or a colorless powder compact for a quick hit to soak up the moisture. You can quickly use these in the restroom or behind the scenes. Just having these in your pocket can minimize the worry about others being aware that you powder your face or having to ask a makeup artist to help you if you are a guest on a show or a featured public speaker. My male clients tell me this has really helped so they can take care of this problem themselves and not draw unwanted attention.

PURPLE CONEFLOWER (ECHINACEA) POWER

Echinacea—commonly known as purple coneflower—is known to defend against colds and flu, so I was excited to find out that a strain called *Echinacea angustifolia* has been shown to be a powerful natural remedy for anxiety, stress, and tension. The root of this strain contains substances that bind to specific brain receptors that tell the body to calm down. Recommended for occasional anxiety associated with public speaking, air travel, interviews, and other stressful events, it's nondrowsy, and only a low dose of approximately 20 mg is needed. Some research indicates that *Echinacea angustifolia* can help with sweating, upset stomach, and trouble sleeping.

CHAMOMILE CUP O' CALM

So many people I know find themselves getting into the habit of coming home after a long day and relaxing with a glass of wine. While studies have shown that one glass of red wine may provide health benefits, the Million Women Study in the United Kingdom shows that even one drink a day can increase the risk of certain cancers. It's also known that just one drink can prevent you from getting the deep, rejuvenating sleep you need. Make naturally caffeine-free chamomile tea your new ritual. I found that it gave me a more soothing, relaxing way to unwind. The process of picking a great mug or cup, steeping the tea, and slowly sipping the warmth is much more relaxing than getting buzzed. The bonus as you shut off the lights is deeper, longer blocks of sleep and no weight gain. I bring chamomile tea on business trips and everywhere I go. It's a "cup of calm" any time of the day.

Calmfidence Seeds of Success

SUNFLOWER POWER

High in magnesium, sunflower seeds have long had a reputation for helping people relax and keep calm. Many performers carry them to control nerves, ease stress, and even help with migraines. They also contain high levels of vitamin E, which brings a youthful glow to your skin.

WHEN YOUR ADRENALINE LEADS, REACH FOR CHIA SEEDS

Chia seeds are the edible seeds of *Salvia hispanica*, a flowering plant in the sage family. Chia seeds contain magnesium, an essential mineral for managing stress, and also have high levels of Omega-3 fatty acids, which bring anti-inflammatory benefits to the brain to lower stress and anxiety. Pop them in an energy drink, cereal, salad, or yogurt as a secret stress buster.

Calming Foods

GET PICKLED

A study conducted by researchers at the University of Maryland showed a connection between eating pickled foods and feeling less anxious. The findings published in the August 2015 issue of *Psychiatry Research* followed the dietary habits of seven hundred college students. Those who had a habit of eating foods like sauerkraut, kimchi, and pickles had less social anxiety and were less moody. So, if you feel like you're in a pickle . . . eat one!

FEEL YOUR OATS

Oatmeal helps get your calm-inducing hormone serotonin flowing. The thick-cut, old-fashioned oats that require cooking work even better than instant oatmeal. Coarse oats are higher in fiber, so they take longer to digest, which makes their calming effect last even longer. When you need to launch your day with calm Calmfidence, a bowl of oatmeal—perhaps topped with ground cinnamon and cardamom and chia seeds—is your surefire Calmfidence meal.

PARSLEY POWER

Usually discarded as decoration, parsley contains high amounts of the compound apigenin, which reduces anxiety by increasing the activity of monoamine transporters. These transporters reduce the amount of stimulation activating the nervous system, which we experience as anxiety, so when this stimulation is slowed, we feel more relaxed. Parsley also has a high mineral content. Minerals are needed to produce the amino acid precursors to calming neurotransmitters and to transmit nerve signals in the brain to keep your mood more stable. Chew on raw parsley for an added bonus of fresher breath, or add it to smoothies, soups, and salads before that big date, meeting, or event.

STALKING CALMFIDENCE

Research shows that celery contains the same calming apigenin that parsley does, and celery has a long history as an anxiety and insomnia remedy. Chewing in general helps to reduce cortisol levels, calm our nerves, and unlock a stressed tight jaw. So, chewing on crisp crunchy celery could be the best form of stress eating there is. Another bonus: apigenin is a potent anticancer compound. Celery also contains magnesium and calcium, both of which have a relaxing effect on the nervous system, and has been shown to help with acid reflux. Because of its high water content, celery can help keep you hydrated to avoid dry mouth and coated tongue. Plus, it's portable. You can take it with you just about anywhere with no mess or fuss.

DROP YOUR SUGAR DADDY

This one is a DON'T: don't sugarcoat your food! Your mom and your dentist have most likely already told you that sugar isn't good for your skin, waistline, teeth, and blood-sugar levels. Sugar can also mess with your ability to handle stress and anxiety. It can affect your mood and aggravate depression. Sugar can even cause difficulty thinking, blurred vision, and make you feel fatigued. You might confuse these symptoms with the onset of a panic attack, leaving you with unnecessary worry that one is about to happen. Sugar can also compromise abilities like learning and memory. If you experience stage fright, public-speaking fear, or lack Calmfidence in any situation, the last thing you need is something to aggravate your mood. Working to eliminate sugar from your diet can help you get a handle on stress and anxiety. You'll boost your natural energy level and feel less agitated and more balanced. This is especially important leading up to any event where the spotlight is on you and Calmfidence is key.

Working these foods and natural remedies into your diet before a big day or stressful event can help you feel more calm and confident. It's also reassuring to know that you have some natural tricks up your sleeve that can be your own little secret stashes of calm when you need them in your Calmfidence arsenal. Now it's time to move on to the next step in our natural Calmfidence journey with chapter 17, "Calmfidence Exercises." Don't worry, this isn't the *working out* kind of exercise. The tips in the next chapter will cover some effective mental exercises and relaxation techniques used by many professional speakers and performers. Let's go!

17

Calmfidence Exercises

Many of the professional speakers, performers, and executives I work with enjoy utilizing the mental exercises and relaxation techniques I give them to manage the stress and adrenaline that comes with being in the spotlight. I'll discuss a dozen of my favorites in the following pages.

The Snow Globe Exercise

Mark Thornton, author of *Meditation in a New York Minute*, teaches busy corporate executives how to meditate in small effective doses. Mark taught me how to use The Snow Globe technique as a quick way to calm the mind. I've used this approach with many clients over the years, recommending they do it back stage, in the bathroom, down the hall, or at the water cooler, in order to clear their heads and solidify a positive game plan just before a big moment. Meditation can be as simple as taking thirty seconds to two minutes to just let the snow globe of your mind settle. Just close your eyes, breathe deeply, picture your mind as that shaken snow globe, and watch it settle and clear. Then picture what you want to have happen next.

Only envision positive outcomes. This will have a big positive impact on whatever situation you are about to go into. You'll have a better handle on things because you will be calmer and more focused.

Remember, if you can work yourself up into a stressed-out state with your actions, thoughts, and self-talk, then the opposite has to be true—you can work yourself down off the roof by quieting your body and mind and changing what you say to yourself. Once you master small doses of the *inside job*, you'll be able to delve deeper into longer sessions with yourself and look forward to making a time and place for them.

The Sack of Potatoes Relaxation Technique

Years ago, I met a big, bold Southern businessman in a ten-gallon cowboy hat who was a successful CEO of a large company. Charming and outgoing, he also was under enormous pressures. Thousands of families' livelihoods rested on this man and the decisions he made every day. I asked him how he kept so calm and optimistic with so much responsibility, and he taught me about his "Sack of Potatoes" daily ritual.

Every afternoon he would close the door to his office and fall back into his chair as if his body had no bones at all. He would then picture his body as a big sack of potatoes. Then at his feet he would envision cutting open the bottom of the sack with a pair of mental scissors and allowing all the potatoes to fall out around him onto the floor. By doing this for just a few minutes he would allow every muscle in his body to relax, and the stress would pour out of him onto the ground. I tried it, and it works. I still use this exercise, and now many of my clients do as well.

Facial Relaxation

Just like a singer or voice-over artist warms up their voice before an audition or performance, you can warm up your face before a speech, meeting, or interview so that you feel less tension in your jaw and facial muscles and feel more in tune with how you are communicating nonverbally. Here are a few tricks used by actors, television presenters, and seasoned public speakers:

- The Pumpkin Raisin: If you do this in front of a mirror or in front of others, you might feel a bit silly, but it works! Keeping your lips closed tightly, fill your mouth with as much air as possible like a blowfish. Hold for three seconds. Now while keeping your lips closed tight suck back in all that air so your cheeks become hollow and your lips purse tight as if you just tasted a sour lemon or were trying to hold a raisin between your lips. Hold for three seconds. Alternate between the two for about 8–10 reps. This will loosen up your face, get the circulation moving, and maybe even help you laugh at yourself a bit.

- The Basset Hound: Close your eyes and envision your entire face pulled down to the floor by gravity. Let it all hang and droop, allowing all of your facial muscles to relax. Slowly count to ten. Open your eyes, then repeat two or three times, depending on how much tension you were holding in your face and jaw.

- The Hang Over: Bend forward with your hands on the floor or on a low table or chair. Let your head hang upside down, relaxing your facial muscles. This is like the Basset Hound only inverted. Feel the blood rush to your scalp and face. Count to five, then come back up. Repeat two more times. This will relax your face and also your scalp, where many people hold a lot of tension. A bonus side effect—rosy cheeks!

- The Pinch Hitter: Gently pinch your cheeks, your jawline, your chin, nose, lips, and eyebrows. This will wake up your muscles, get blood flowing, massage out some tension, and give you a healthy glow.

The Mammalian Diving Reflex

You've probably heard that splashing cold water on your face or taking a cold shower can help wake you up, snap you out of it, or refresh you. Cold water on your face can actually slow your heart rate during a surge of adrenaline or stage fright. You can thank the mammalian diving reflex for this. It's a reflex in mammals that optimizes our respiration so we can stay underwater for extended periods of time to increase our chance of survival when needed. It's utilized in aquatic mammals like seals and dolphins and also occasionally in other mammals, including humans. As soon as your face hits water below 70 degrees F, your heart rate slows down 10–25 percent!

I admit, clients who are wearing makeup or are dressed to impress don't want to splash cold water on their faces right before a TV appearance or big presentation—so I recommend using an ice pack, a frozen bag of veggies, an ice cube wrapped in a napkin, or a cold towel or compress instead. By holding it against your cheeks, forehead, chin, and area around the nose for a few minutes, you can activate the trigeminal and vagus nerves, which will cause your pulse rate to drop and quickly calm your nerves. An added bonus is that it can minimize puffiness under your eyes and even give a rosy glow to your cheeks!

Chime In

The calming sound of wind chimes can release stress, improve your focus, calm your mind, and create an instant relaxing environment. Wind chimes increase creativity and give you inspiration. They can be a peaceful way to fall asleep, and also to wake up to, to start off your day in a positive way. Some people believe that wind chimes help enhance the mind/body/spirit connection, giving us a sense of well-being. If you can't hang wind chimes where you are—for example, in your office or on the road—playing a wind chime video or sound recording on your phone or other device can have a similar effect on your body and mind.

Get Stoned

Worry stones, stress stones, or pocket stones—however you refer to them, they work. Rubbing a stone repetitively keeps your sensory inputs busy, relieves stress and anxiety, gets rid of excess energy, keeps you calm, and grounds you.

Stones inscribed with simple affirmations will remind you of your goal, a positive thought, or intention. There are many colors, textures, and sizes. Have fun picking just the right one for you, to keep in your pocket, briefcase, purse, or desk. This can be your secret little ritual that no one else sees—or a conversation starter if you carry it in the palm of your hand. Try it out before your next big meeting, interview, presentation, or event.

Chew on It

Studies show that chewing gum can help relieve stress, increase your focus and recall, and even get you in a more positive mood. The repetitive chewing motion can soothe your nerves while also helping to counteract dry mouth, a coated tongue, and a tight jaw—all of which can happen simultaneously when you are in a nerve-wracking situation. I chew gum right up until I go live on the air, before I give a speech, when I'm writing, and before interviews. My clients do the same, and they tell me it really helps. Just be sure to ditch it before you start talking. Gum chewing and clear oral communication just don't mix.

Calming Candlelight

Studies show the simple act of lighting a candle and watching its glow can relieve stress and calm your spirit. Couple that with candle scents like calming lavender and lemon, which can lower cortisol, for a powerful effect. I love small candles that come in tins because they're portable. You can bring them to the office, on a business trip, or anywhere else you want to create a calming effect so you can center yourself before that big meeting, interview, or event.

DIY Acupressure

The human body responds dramatically to touch. It's a great stress reliever that can help us relax. It reassures us and connects us. It can help us grow and even help us heal. Some of my clients are blessed with a support staff that includes massage therapy prior to appearances or events. But if you can't take a personal masseuse with you to stressful or high-stakes situations, there are many acupressure and massage tricks you can do yourself. Keep in mind that most of these tricks can be viewed as self-soothing body language "tells"—nonverbal signs that could send a message to others that you are dealing with stress or anxiety—so you'll want to do them alone, prior to and not during any interaction where you want to come across as cool and full of Calmfidence.

- Eyebrow rub and press: it's amazing how much stress we hold in and over our eyebrows. The eyebrows are one of the most expressive parts of our face, and those muscles sure do get a workout when we are concentrating, worrying, or primed for action. By using your thumb and pointer finger to rub and squeeze your eyebrows you can give those muscles a mini vacation. Pressing your thumb and pointer finger simultaneously to your forehead just slightly above both eyebrows and holding for a few seconds releases tension and can even lessen a stress headache.

- Use your thumb to press the soft spot on your other hand between your thumb and pointer finger. This can help ease head and neck pain.

- Rub your earlobes. This acupressure trick dulls pain above the neck and increases alertness.

- Press and rub your jaw and chin. Many people grind their teeth and clench their jaw unconsciously when they have stage fright or fear public speaking. This will relax your face and make it easy to open your mouth and speak your mind.

- The H-7 pressure point: press your thumb on the pulse point on your other wrist. Hold for one minute while breathing deeply. This acupressure point relieves anxiety, nervousness, fear, and forgetfulness.

Secret Stress Release

If you have nervous energy, anxiety, or any other emotion that you want to relieve without anyone noticing, one simple thing you can do is to squeeze your toes! This is a great stealth move because you can squeeze, wiggle, or stretch those toes anytime and no one will know what you are up to. Not only does this feel good, it's a great distraction that takes your mind off any other physical feelings you might be experiencing, like a pounding heart. This can secretly replace other more obvious self-soothing habits or pacifying self-touch gestures.

Furry Calmfidence

I use this one daily with my three shih-tzus! Pet therapy is used to help people recover from illness and surgeries in hospitals, nursing homes, and rehabilitation centers. Pets help people cope with all kinds of health problems, from heart disease and cancer to mental health issues including stress and anxiety. A little fur therapy also works to bring some relief to your stage fright, presentation jitters, salary negotiation knee-knocking, and speaking up to that arrogant coworker. Pets help us to be in the moment. They provide unconditional love with no judgment. The rhythmic action of petting a furry friend can sooth your nerves and calm your body, mind, and spirit. If you can bring Fido or Fluffy to work, even better. Many studies show that pets increase feelings of happiness, boost energy levels, and remind us of what's truly important. Other studies show that even just looking at a picture of your beloved pet can help calm your nerves, soothe your soul, and distract you from negative thinking or fearful thoughts. So right before you walk into that big interview, onto that stage, or into any nerve-wracking situation, pull out a picture of your furry friend, feel some instant love and calm, and smile.

Create a Calmfidence Emergency Port-a-Pack

We've all heard the saying "Make sure your bags are packed." It basically means, be sure you are prepared for life's little or big emergencies. If the thought of public speaking, appearing in front of a camera, communicating with others, or dealing with a confrontational situation falls under the category of *emergency situation* for you, be sure your Calmfidence emergency port-a-pack is ready to go. Designate a soft lunch box or small travel bag and fill it with some or all of these fast-working Calmfidence-inducing goodies:

- Lemon balm extract
- Small gel ice packs
- Banana
- Lavender oil or cream

- Citrus perfume
- Dried cherries
- Your Calmfidence credit card (chapter 6)
- Chewing gum
- Chamomile tea bags
- Essential oils
- Cinnamon sticks
- Sunflower seeds
- A small stress squeeze ball
- A small smooth rubbing stone
- A religious trinket or symbol if you are a person of faith

EPILOGUE

We all walk in the dark and each of us must
learn to turn on his or her own light.

Earl Nightingale

Back in 2008, I had just come off my best year ever, traveling the country as a television spokesperson for a fashion brand. Then the perfect storm hit—first, the crash and recession of 2008. Then I lost two regular TV programs I had hosted for over ten years. I was fighting with my husband, worrying over finances and our different approaches to parenting our only child. We were going through infertility treatments, desperately trying to have a sibling for our son without any success. My father was ill. My whole world was in disarray.

I had a meltdown. The anxiety and depression became something that I couldn't manage with my normal positive thinking, self-care, and exercise. I couldn't sleep, and because I had trouble swallowing, I couldn't eat. I lost weight and looked ill. I had to admit that I needed professional help. The doctor's recommendation was to go on medication, which scared me, but finally agreeing to take that medication was the very thing that broke the vicious cycle I could not break on my own. I started to sleep and eat better and function more normally.

As I started to share my experience with friends and family, to my surprise many people admitted that they too were on some kind of anti-anxiety or anti-depression medication. These people all seemed to be coping well with few worries, but I learned that we were all struggling with something. And we all need help at some point.

After six months on the medication, I felt better, work picked back up, and things got better for me. That experience gave me so much empathy and compassion for people who are struggling with mental health issues. It showed me that it's so important for everyone to openly discuss them and to be supportive of people seeking help—and to allow ourselves to ask for help, too.

Two years later I found myself in the anchor chair of an international morning show and live noon broadcast. This then led to a national American network anchor job, which I had always aimed for, although it turned out that that network was not a good fit for me and I handed in my resignation. While I had maintained my coaching and training business, it had dwindled because of my intense anchor schedule, so I had to reinvent once again; it took a good year to build my business back up.

I tell you all of this because you may be in the middle of your own Calmfidence journey right now. You may be dealing with stress and anxiety, problems with work, depression, or other illness. You're not alone.

I think it's important for you to know that my Calmfidence was once again put to the test as I wrote this book (my first!), and so it was a new experience for me. I simultaneously loved and doubted my way through each chapter. I would tell people about the book I was writing just to hear if it was something they would actually read. I gave speeches, workshops, and television interviews based on my Calmfidence concepts, stories, and tips. As I talked about the book to anyone who would listen, the feedback was the same: *I'd read that! I could really use a book like that!* My heart would glow and I'd find new determination to continue writing.

My dad always encouraged me and helped me build my Calmfidence in different ways over the years, though he never really had much of his own. Dad worked at thankless jobs where he didn't speak up for himself. He would have great business ideas and created beautiful paintings and sculptures, and yet he always stopped short of sending them out into the world. A US Marine who attended New York University after World War II, he never finished, stopping just a few credits shy of his degree. It was one of his biggest regrets, which made him feel *less than*, even though he devoured hundreds of books over the years and had a deep knowledge of history, religious studies, art, science, and aeronautics. He was the smartest man I knew, and I could ask him anything—he was Google before there was Google. But he didn't believe in *himself*. At his funeral, my uncle came up to me to tell me how proud the family was that I was one of the first to "break through the confidence barrier" that plagued a good portion of my relatives.

I wrote this final section of the book on what would have been my dad's ninetieth birthday. A man of deep faith, he did experience total Calmfidence and conviction at one incredible moment: in the hospital right before he passed away. He smiled at my mom and me and said, "I'm going on the greatest journey of my life." He meant it, and we believed him.

I know that my father would want me to share everything I've learned with as many people as possible. So, this book is for you. My wish for you is that you embrace the concepts in this book, grab hold of your inner critic and silence it, and build the courage to trust yourself to speak your mind, pursue your dreams, and live life to the fullest, loving every crazy minute of it, with all the Calmfidence you can create for yourself.

Acknowledgments

A heartfelt thank-you to my literary agent, Leslie Meredith, and to Haven Iverson and the team at Sounds True for believing in my work and helping me in so many ways to bring Calmfidence to life. Thank you to Christine Baker and Glenn Lewis for encouraging me to stay on track, get unstuck, and find my "why" during the early days of my writing. Thank you, Debby Englander, for all of your guidance, input, and assistance. Thank you to my mother and father, who helped me develop my own Calmfidence over the years; to my husband, Brian, who has always been my best friend, supporter, and Calmfidence booster; and to my son, Logan, for being the best son a mother could ever ask for, and for never complaining when I made you my Calmfidence project with all of my endless well-meaning lessons. Thank you to my sister Kathy for all of her encouragement. To Dara, Jimmy, Shannon, Brittany, and Madison for always being the best family a person could hope for and for being there throughout the journey.

Thanks too to all my PRHS girls—my lifelong friends—and my South Orangetown girls for all your love and support, and to Danielle Young for all your assistance and insight. To my wonderful women of AWE, Michele Phillips and Dr. Lisa Brooks Greaux, for all of your love, support, and encouragement. To dear friends Janetlee, Katie, Eber, Paula, Ginny, and Annie for your friendship, creative eye, and love. I thank God for always being my pilot, guiding me and walking with me on this path. Thank you to all my students and clients, whom I have learned so much from over the years.

About the Author

Patricia Stark is president of Patricia Stark Communications and Calmfidence® Workshops, based in New York City, providing personal and professional development coaching and training focusing on public speaking, media training, virtual presentation training, talent development, body language, emotional intelligence, and peak performance. She has developed effective, concrete strategies that empower clients to take command of their communication skills, minimize stress and anxiety, and overcome fear and self-doubt to build a solid foundation of inner trust. Clients include ESPN, the Smithsonian Institute, NASA TV, Amazon, BET, GAIA, Turner Broadcasting, CBS, CNBC, OWN, NASCAR, Conde Nast, Spotify, Hoover, Quaker Oats, KPMG, the American Medical Association, *Prevention* magazine, Discovery Channel, E! News, Soul Cycle, Martha Stewart Living Omnimedia, Novartis, and The Shark Group.

In front of the camera, Patricia has extensive experience as a health and wellness anchor and television host, virtual meeting moderator, national and international news anchor, performer on *Law & Order: Criminal Intent*, and as a commercial spokesperson for Hoover, Olay, Ovaltine, and Soma. She has also served as a contributor for the History Channel and the Huffington Post, as a talent judge on twenty-six episodes of the Emmy-nominated performing talent show *New York Star of the Day*, and as host/writer of the Calmfidence® for Teens segments on the Emmy Award–winning remake of the children's show *Wonderama*.

Patricia has been interviewed for the *Wall Street Journal's* popular *Secrets of Wealthy Women* podcast, IHeart Radio's award-winning *What Women Want* podcast, CBS News' Small Business Spotlight, *Scholastic* magazine, *New York Lifestyles Magazine*, and NJ PBS - NJTV *One on One*, and is a recurring guest expert on WNYW Fox 5 New York. She is a guest lecturer at colleges and universities on the topics of communication skills,

Calmfidence®, public-speaking skills, interpersonal skills, and interview skills. She currently brings her trademarked Calmfidence® Workshops and keynote speeches to Fortune 500 corporations, nonprofit organizations, teen self-esteem events, and women's leadership conferences.

Patricia is a Certified Body Language Trainer and has earned certificates in eclectic cognitive behavior therapy, visualization and guided imagery counseling, personal and executive coaching, and positive psychology. She is a member of the Screen Actors Guild/American Federation of Television & Radio Artists. She serves as a communications volunteer for Dress for Success, the Diabetes Association, and United Way. Clients have traveled from Saudi Arabia, Japan, Australia, New Zealand, France, The Netherlands, England, and Korea to train with Patricia.

About Sounds True

S ounds True is a multimedia publisher whose mission is to inspire and support personal transformation and spiritual awakening. Founded in 1985 and located in Boulder, Colorado, we work with many of the leading spiritual teachers, thinkers, healers, and visionary artists of our time. We strive with every title to preserve the essential "living wisdom" of the author or artist. It is our goal to create products that not only provide information to a reader or listener but also embody the quality of a wisdom transmission.

For those seeking genuine transformation, Sounds True is your trusted partner. At SoundsTrue.com you will find a wealth of free resources to support your journey, including exclusive weekly audio interviews, free downloads, interactive learning tools, and other special savings on all our titles.

To learn more, please visit SoundsTrue.com/freegifts or call us toll-free at 800.333.9185.